I0476644

CompeteAbility

Your Company's Ability To Create
Competitive Advantage.

2nd Edition

CompeteAbility

Your Company's Ability To Create
Competitive Advantage.

2nd Edition

By
Bill Burnett

CompeteAbility
Your Company's Ability To Create Competitive Advantage.

Copyright © 2015, 2017 by Bill Burnett

ISBN-13: 978-1514339008
ISBN-10: 1514339005

Email:

Give feedback on the book at:
bill@manuparx.com

Acknowledgements

I want to thank Linda, my lovely wife who's been supportive through all my writing and has always been my first editor.

Over nearly five decades of working I've learned from the many great leaders I've had the pleasure of engaging with. I have also learned from those who aspire to lead but manage to completely miss the mark. However, because one's own experiences tend to be less than objective, in this monograph I attempted to base the observations on research. I've incorporated tools that are both backed up by good science and are tried-and-true with thousands of users. I am thankful to all those who have studied the topic contained herein, and who thoughtfully published their stories and findings.

Thank you to the Saturday morning Levy Group who generously provided feedback to me on early versions of this re-write.

Finally, I want to thank Cheryl Kennedy who generously gave her time to edit, and greatly improve the first half of the manuscript, and my son Charles Burnett who turns out to be a phenomenal and very frank editor who worked on the second half. If you need a great editor, I will happily connect you to Cheryl or Charles. Any errors that remain are mine. Please feel free to point them out and I will happily include your name in these acknowledgements in a future printing.

Suppose out of the blue someone says to you, "I can run your business better than you can."

You'd probably be thinking, 'Hold on just a second here. You don't know my business, my products, my people, my industry, my competitors, or me. How could you possibly think you could do this better than me?"

You'd be right of course. That other person might know a bit about your industry and maybe something about a competitor or two, but otherwise wouldn't know anything about your business, and, more importantly, wouldn't have your passion for the business. It's a ridiculous claim. It would not be true that this person could run your business better than you.

But you can!

You are the one person in your business that's in the best

1

position to improve how your business performs.

In this monograph we are going to take a look at a handful of leaders who were in exactly that position. Each of them realized three important things:

1. The opportunity to improve my company performance is substantial.
2. To get there I need every employee to develop a deep sense of ownership in the company.
3. The first thing that needs to change is me.

What matters most to the long term success of companies is their ability to compete. CompeteAbility is about maximizing that ability based on the success of the few organization that have done this extraordinarily well, coupled with research into human behavior and the tools that can smooth the road to success and, ultimately, make such success inevitable.

We will briefly look at what these leaders did. We will also look at some broader data that points in exactly the same direction. The second half of the book is about a step-by-step process that simplifies what you might do to get to much better performance, and how to inject a deep sense of ownership into the people who make up your team.

I magine the audacity of a dozen employees who thought that their pooled one million dollars could purchase the $300 million company. They were up against Goldman Sachs, the investment bank that had been hired to sell the company. To round-out the offer, the employees got Citibank to loan them another $80 million.

Eighty-one million dollars for a $300 million dollar company was a ridiculous offer. But the employees were tenacious, and after months of negotiation, and with no other offer on the table, the deal was done at $81.5 million. For their million-dollar stake, the employees had just bought a motorcycle company called Harley-Davidson. As amazing as this transaction was, the really interesting thing was what the leadership at Harley learned in turning the company around.

At the time of the purchase in 1981, Harley-Davidson was in serious trouble. It was losing market share to its Japanese competitors, particularly Honda. In Harley's market niche, Honda's large street bike, the Gold Wing, had taken a lead

3

in market share, knocking Harley off the top spot it had held for a long time.

Harley had other problems as well: costs and quality. Low quality in the supply chain and shoddy work on the assembly line caused waste and errors. Typical of companies with these problems, Harley responded by setting up a rigorous post-production quality function. It put a huge proportion of finished bikes into its "Hospital" to be repaired and made ready to ship.

The organization was focused on short-term solutions: it maintained high parts inventory levels as a safety net and spent money on technology and state-of-the-art machinery to boost productivity, but didn't focus on design and engineering development.

Most importantly, management did not listen to employees. Despite obvious internal production problems, corporate leadership tended to blame the business decline on competition from foreign manufacturers that they perceived as unfair. (Even today this is a common complaint from companies that haven't figured out how to build and sustain competitive advantage.)

Once the buyout was completed, things got much worse. The Reagan recession hit. One of the first things people stop spending money on in a recession is expensive recreational vehicles. But Harley had one advantage—an extraordinarily loyal customer base. Even though the quality of assembly was poor—the joke was that you could always tell where a Harley had parked by the pool of oil left on the pavement—customers loved their Harley motorcycles.

The new leadership at Harley decided to take the Japanese production methods and use them to beat the Japanese at their own game. They implemented a three-pronged attack. This was no easy task. First, they set up just-in-time-inventory structures. Second, they measured at the employee level every data point that mattered to them. Third, they got their employees fully engaged in building for quality.

The dedication of employees was the most important lesson identified by Richard Teerlink Harley Davidson's chief executive officer at the time. Without that dedication the company would have no long-term success. According to Teerlink top management has the responsibility and an obligation to create the right environment where every employee is free to challenge the system in the pursuit of success. Other production techniques and tools become easy once the employee is committed."[1]

The biggest obstacle to Harley's recovery in 1981 was its management. At first, quality remained a purview of management. But quality remained low. Then, management saw that the employees who built the product didn't want low quality leaving the factory, so they started the long process of moving ownership of quality to plant floor workers and giving them the tools they needed to achieve the outstanding quality Harley-Davidson motorcycles are known for today.[2]

The company also found ways to greatly improve

[1] Peter C. Reid, Well Made in America: Lessons from Harley-Davidsons on Being the Best, McGraw-Hill, New York, 1990, P. 7
[2] Ibid. P. 75

productivity. They realized that automating a process that's inefficient to begin with simply gives you an inefficient automated process. Fortunately for Harley, the company didn't have the cash to invest in automation. Instead, management redesigned the work into work cells where a worker was able to perform all the operations in the same location. In some cases, a single worker built the whole part. This turns out to be personally gratifying to an employee because he or she has 'ownership' of the product.[3]

It was a successful turnaround. Inventories dropped 75%, productivity increased 50%, waste dropped 68%[4], U.S. revenues jumped 80%, and the much improved quality and design even caused international sales to jump 177%. Most notably, with a 97% lift in share, Harley regained the top market spot, displacing Honda. And, of course, the company became quite profitable.

3 Ibid. P. 142
4 Ibid. P. 148

Introduction

"**C**an we possibly conclude that it's working?" Professor Michael Porter asked as he stood before an amphitheater of economic development professionals in Minneapolis and condemned the four main activities his audience had been engaged in for the past 20 years. "I don't think so. We now have to give up on these things."

The renowned Harvard Business School professor had argued that making the region business-friendly, entering bidding wars to attract relocating businesses, trying to create a new cluster of the "next big" industry, and investing in industrial zones or incubators were either just table stakes, or of low or no value to the regional economy.[5]

So what did Porter think these folks should be doing to develop their regional economy?

5 "Superinnovators: Michael Porter Takes Regional Economic Development to Task." WBurnett LLC, 13 Oct. 2014. Web. 23 Feb. 2015. <http://superinnovator.blogspot.com/2014/10/michael-porter-takes-regional-economic.html>.

He put forth these two ideas:
1. Focus on competitiveness.
2. Build an environment where employees can be highly productive and innovative.

Porter's suggestion to this audience applies even more to running a business. These two ideas enable a business to become the competitive powerhouse that's often locked away by how the company operates.

Focus on Competitiveness

Good economists know that the source of new money into an economy is business. That's it. There is no other significant source of economic growth in any economy anywhere in the world. The health of an economy depends upon the health of its businesses. We cannot respond to Porter's challenge to focus on competitiveness without addressing it at the individual company level.

Every business CEO knows that the long-term health of a business depends on competitive advantage.[6] It is found through:

Product (or service) functionality
Packaging
Marketing
Pricing

---

6 While this monograph is about competitive advantage, the approach makes it far more likely that a blue ocean initiative will be successful because it helps leaders eliminate the biggest obstacle to blue ocean success: ingrained assumptions and theories that create company and industry dogma.

Selling
Servicing
Enhancing the customer's sense of identity
Having the customer find greater meaning
Causing the customer to like and respect your company

These are the key factors of "competeability," your company's ability to compete.

Many of your competitors will respond to Porter's call to "focus" by identifying one or two of these areas of competitive advantage and putting their energies there. They won't completely ignore the other factors, but they also won't attend to them as though they were critical to making the company as competitive as possible. Many business gurus promote this definition of "focus."

That's not how Robert Galvin thought about it. He ran Motorola back when it was a remarkably successful company. Galvin once said that managers often say things like, "We can only support so many new initiatives." Or, "There will always be projects on our cut-off list." Or, "There are only so many good people." Or, "We can't do everything." Galvin called these roadblock statements.

True leaders, said Galvin, don't make roadblock statements. Instead, they ask, "How do we...?" questions. "How do we support every initiative? How do we keep every project alive? They're all good people, how do we make them great? Or, how can we do everything?" Galvin recognized that companies still wouldn't undertake every possible initiative, but felt strongly that leaders can accomplish a lot more by starting with a "How do we…?" question instead of a roadblock.

9

Successful business leaders define "focus" as Galvin would. They understand "focus" as concentration on all of these factors of competeability. They have figured out the answer to the question, "How do we concentrate on all of them?"

Such leaders also know that the key activity in creating and maintaining competitive advantage is problem solving. They ask, "How do we create a solution that does the job better than the competition?" It's an over arching theme under which other questions of competitive advantage fall:

- How do we maintain the strongest possible relationship with the customer?
- How do we package our solution better than the competition?
- How do we market our solution better than the competition?
- How do we price our solution better than the competition?
- How do we sell our solution better than the competition?
- How do we service our solution better than the competition?
- How do we get the customer to feel kinship with us through our solution?
- How do we give the customer identity through our solution?
- How do we create meaning for the customer through our solution?

These are all problems that need to be solved. Solve them better than your competition in the eyes of the customer, and you win the business.

Who should solve these competeability problems, and how many people should engage in solving them?

As CEO you employ people to solve these problems all day, every day. And if they are not solving some kind of problem, what are they doing?

If it's competitive advantage you're looking for, understand that it is everyone who works for you who should be creating competitive advantage. Every employee should be contributing to solving one or more of the "how do we...?" questions above.[7]

Build an Environment Where Employees Can be Highly Productive and Innovative

Innovation is simply a form of problem solving. It involves creating new knowledge or using existing knowledge in a different way.

How do you build an environment where your people can be highly productive and innovative, where they can be great problem solvers, out-produce the competition, and deliver the highest quality work?

---

7 If you have employees who are performing functions that do not address at least one of these competeability problems, then their functions are candidates for outsourcing. If you are outsourcing functions that do address any of these problems, then those are candidates for insourcing.

Lean In, Leave Out

I f you google "lean production practices," you will get a list of results that includes concepts like:

- Kaizen - continuous improvement
- JIT - just-in-time manufacturing
- Muda - waste reduction
- RCA - root cause analysis
- SMART goals
- Value stream mapping
- Visual workplace
- Bottleneck analysis
- PDCA - plan-do-check-act

If you had to rank these according to which has the most impact on productivity and quality according to the foundational research on lean production, what would be number one?

Surprisingly, the correct answer is "none of the above."

There is something in the foundation of the lean production system that gets lost in our thirst for methods and techniques, but it is the key to answering the question "How do we build the right environment for creating competitive advantage?"

John F. Krafcik,[8] then an MBA candidate at MIT's Sloan School of Management coined the term 'Lean Production System' in 1988. That year, Krafcik published a paper in the MIT Sloan Management Review entitled "Triumph of the Lean Production System."[9]

At the time, Krafcik was the lead researcher in the MIT International Motor Vehicle Program study of assembly plants around the world. The premise behind the research suggested that companies enjoy a decided competitive advantage where they combine high productivity, high quality, and high product flexibility. Krafcik and his colleagues sought a set of tools that would allow the accurate identification of the best manufacturing practices Krafcik and his research partner built a mechanism to enable them to deliver a comprehensive comparative analysis based on their visits to 38 assembly plants in 13 countries.[10]

The above list of lean production practices would suggest that the key finding from Krafcik's research is that the

8 After earning an engineering degree at Stanford and before pursuing his MBA at MIT, Krafcik had worked as a manufacturing engineer at the NUMMI plant, a GM-Toyota joint venture in California. He eventually became CEO of Hyundai America.
9 Available at: http://www.lean.org/downloads/MITSloan.pdf
10 John F. Krafcik, Comparative Analysis of Performance Indicators at World Auto Assembly Plants, unpublished master's thesis at the Alfred P. Sloan School of Management MIT, January 1988.

determinant of high productivity and quality is the application of some combination of these processes. But the research pointed to something different.

Toyota is the source of many of the concepts that were the foundation of Krafcik's Lean Production System. When Krafcik worked at the NUMMI plant in Fremont, California before going to MIT for his MBA, he'd been exposed to many of these ideas. But a number of observers have noted that while the Toyota Production System has been credited with Toyota's productivity and quality successes, it turns out that very few manufacturers have been able to imitate Toyota successfully. This despite the company's willingness to be extraordinarily open about its practices.[11]

Some have suggested that the Japanese culture enables Toyota to enjoy such production success. But research by Krafcik and others showed that other Japanese companies failed to achieve Toyota's standards, while Toyota had transplanted its success into other national cultures in many parts of the world.

What was it about Toyota that made it different? In a 1999 Harvard Business Review article, Steven Spear and Kent Bowen found that Toyota did not use a command and control management structure. In observing Toyota workers performing their jobs, they learned that the Toyota management system actually stimulates both employees and their bosses to engage in experimentation. It's an activity widely recognized as the linchpin of a learning organization. That distinguished Toyota from all the other

11 Steven Spear, H. Kent Bowen, Decoding the DNA of the Toyota Production System. Harvard Business Review, September 1999

companies they'd studied.[12]

Krafcik reported in his MIT master's thesis that the independent variable that stood out as the key predictor of productivity was what he called the 'Management Index,' or the production management policy (i.e., how you deal with people). As a predictor, it was significant at the 99% level (much higher than any of the other independent variables). Krafcik concluded that more than anything else, what matters in determining productivity is how you deal with your people.

Krafcik's study also examined determinants of quality and found that the same independent variable, how you deal with people, was the key predictor of success at a 98% level. Krafcik's research partner, J.P. MacDuffie, later noted that the important factor in determining plant performance was how direct labor employees are managed.[13]

The findings from Krafcik's research suggest that it would be a good idea to find out how people work together in the most successful companies. And while it's a hard thing to measure, that doesn't mean we don't have something to learn by looking at such companies.

It is very tempting to start by looking at Toyota. After all, it didn't start out with practices like kaizen or JIT. Something in the way that Toyota managed its people early-on enabled its people to develop these practices. Sakichi Toyoda, Toyota's founder, ran the company in a particular

12 Ibid. p.
13 Steve Babson, Editor: Lean work empowerment and exploitation in the global auto industry, Chapter 9: "The International Assembly Plant Study: Philosophical And Methodological Issues". John Paul MacDuffie And Frits K. Pil, P. 190

way, which later became codified as Toyota's Way.[14] Its five tenets are:

1. Be contributive to the development and welfare of the country by working together, regardless of position, in faithfully fulfilling your duties.
2. Be at the vanguard of the times through endless creativity, inquisitiveness, and pursuit of improvement.
3. Be practical and avoid frivolity.
4. Be kind and generous; strive to create a warm, homelike atmosphere.
5. Be reverent, and show gratitude for things great and small in thought and deed.

When Toyoda said, "create a warm, homelike atmosphere," he meant it literally. Toyoda would often come to the factory early on cold mornings to light the fire in the stoves that warmed the building before other team members arrived for work.[15] Toyota was a people-focused company.

The research that led to the Lean Production System was funded by the automobile industry. As a consequence, it limited itself to just that industry. Had Krafcik been able to include the Harley experience in the MIT study on lean production, he might have been able to zoom in more prescriptively on what really drives productivity and quality, and thus competitive advantage. One has to wonder whether a clearer picture might have emerged

14 Toyota. "Toyoda Precepts: The base of the Global Vision." Toyota. Toyota. April 2012. http://www.toyota-global.com/company/toyota_traditions/company/apr_2012.html (accessed Oct 23, 2012).
15 "Toyoda Precepts: The Base of the Global Vision." Toyota Global Site. N.p., 2012. Web. 03 Feb. 2015. <http://www.toyota-global.com/company/toyota_traditions/company/apr_2012.html>.

if the research had included even more industries. This takes us back to our question, "How do we create an environment that fosters competitive advantage?"

To answer Michael Porter's call to build an environment where we can be highly productive and innovative, we will look beyond the well-studied automobile assembly plant and to companies in other industries that have each done an extraordinary job of creating such an environment.

This is a look at a handful of cases where the leadership has maximized the problem solving contributions of all their people.

The Radio

Now let's go 90 miles south of Harley-Davidson to Schaumburg, Illinois. At the time John Krafcik was submitting his master's thesis in the late 1980s, Robert Galvin was wrapping up a 30-year career as CEO of Motorola. Galvin's insights would have been useful in answering the question of how to build an environment where people can be highly productive and innovative.

In many ways, Motorola under Galvin was the Apple of its day. The company's capacity for innovation was legendary, extending from products such as handheld two-way radios, color televisions, the first cell phone, and a host of network technologies to manufacturing and quality innovations including process improvement methodology Six Sigma. "That's one small step for man, one giant leap for mankind," came to us through Motorola technology.

When Galvin took over from his father, Paul Galvin, Motorola was already a successful company with $217 million in sales. During his tenure at the helm, the junior Galvin and his team added another $217 million in sales on average every year, growing the company to $6.7 billion. Galvin was once asked if there was any one thing he could point to that his father instilled in him as his motivation. He replied, "Yes, my father treated me to the most demanding discipline. He trusted me! This is the highest respect that one person can give to another. It is the most demanding motivator. One does not dare let the other person down."[16]

Galvin understood something very fundamental about building an engine for competitive advantage. When asked what made Motorola successful, he described it as a focus on engaging the minds of the collective "we," as he called it. The leadership supported the development of a <u>very high proportion of employee ideas</u>[17], in a culture where truth was paramount. Trust is crucial in an environment of truth.

Galvin was a proponent of listening for and choosing ideas, but also for listening for the other point of view. "One of the things that we encouraged was that there would be a more than adequacy of minority reports... we'd go back and say 'Who didn't get heard?' or 'who got lost from being identified?' Then that gave us another iteration, since maybe we had been too short-sighted."[18] When a team was congealing around a particular solution, Galvin would watch for the engineer in the back of the room who was shaking his head. That was the engineer

---

16 Robert Galvin, The Idea of Ideas, Motorola University Press, Schaumburg, IL 1991 P. 11

17 In a 2013 survey of over 100,000 companies, Gary Kunkle of Inc. magazine found that the top 100 companies, the 'Build 100' were highly innovative and got their best ideas from within - 90% from individual employees.

18 Robert Galvin, an oral history conducted in 1993 by William Aspray, IEEE History Center, Rutgers University, New Brunswick, NJ, U.S.A.

with the minority report. Later, Galvin would approach that engineer and get his or her point of view. Often enough, that's where he found the best insights.

Galvin had tremendous faith in people. He recognized that in many aspects of their lives, both inside and outside of work, people are leaders. He said, "Reaching out to the leadership qualities that all people possess to a larger degree than traditionally appreciated...Of this I feel confident, our people at all levels of responsibility will rarely be found wanting as the appreciation of their qualities are more evidently invited and trusted. My father [Paul Galvin] urged us to reach out. The idea of reaching out to people—all the people—for their leadership contribution, yes, their creative leadership contribution is the most rewarding potential reach of all."[19]

Central to Motorola's ability to create a "generous share of new products...to be among the first to market these new products," was the company's approach to risk. "There has been a high spirit of risk and commitment to what needs to be done on the part of the we's." To help control the risks around developing new products and technologies, Motorola put in place a process that allowed its scientists and engineers working with other interests in the firm to develop ideas "quicker, better, moving earlier into production, providing better yields." And, like all firms that sustain competitive advantage, they maintained a high degree of integrity in all customer dealings.

Galvin relied on the vast creative, scientific, and engineering capability within Motorola to generate the bulk of ideas.

19 Robert Galvin, The Idea of Ideas, Motorola University Press, Schaumburg, IL, 1991, p.65

The two key factors of "we" are to include everyone's ability to solve problems and to foster an appetite for risks.

Galvin's appetite for risk was broad. He was one of the first to recognize the market potential of China, and managed to convince the Chinese early on to let Motorola start to manufacture there. They insisted, however, that Motorola instruct its Chinese employees and suppliers how to make the high quality products Motorola sold globally. Galvin understood that slowly but surely the Chinese would copy everything Motorola built there. But he calculated that the Chinese market would be so large that the slice left over for Motorola would be plenty big, and he agreed to the condition.

True to his word, Galvin brought to China the manufacture of Motorola's best technology and strict manufacturing quality standards. Motorola's local suppliers eventually spread the company's technology and techniques to second- and third-tier suppliers across China. Using this technology, China built a telecommunication infrastructure that leapfrogged the U.S. It is safe to say that Motorola did more than any other foreign enterprise to create a competitive Chinese industrial capability.[20]

---

20 Ted Fishman, What Happened to Motorola: How a culture shift nearly doomed an iconic local company that once dominated the telecom industry. Chicago Magazine, Aug 25, 2014, http://www.chicagomag.com/Chicago-Magazine/September-2014/What-Happened-to-Motorola/ accessed 1/6/2015

Pumped Up

This chapter takes us to another part of the world, and to a company that was changing how it operated at the same time MIT was doing its "Lean" research. Semco Partners is a Brazilian company owned by Ricardo Semler. Its roots go back to his father's troubled marine pump business. When Ricardo took over Semco it had $4 million in revenue and 90 employees. He was 21 years old.[21]

Semler worked tirelessly to turn the company around. His management team used classical authoritarian, command and control solutions, with rigid oversight, and long, grueling hours. For example, Semler devised a tardiness policy that docked an employee's pay if he was a few minutes late to work. He and his managers were at work early in the morning, and often stayed late into the night. Not surprisingly, the team achieved some success and managed to turn the company around.

21 Chuck Blakeman, Why 'Participation Age' Leaders Will Beat Old-School Managers, Every Time, Inc. Sept, 2014 http://www.inc.com/chuck-blakeman/marissa-mayer-the-old-school-manager-vs-ricardo-semler-the-participation-age-lea.html

However, on a trip to a pump factory in Baldwinsville, New York, Semler suddenly felt ill and passed out. As it was the second time this had happened to him, the local doctor sent him to the Lahey Clinic in Boston where, for three days, doctors ran all sorts of tests. The diagnosis was simple: there was nothing physically wrong with 25 year old Semler except an advanced case of stress. He was told, he could either continue his existing lifestyle, in which case he'd be back in the hospital, or he could change.[22]

Semler was already troubled by what he had observed in his factories. Particularly distressing to him was that workers just didn't seem to care. He began to make changes. First, he tackled his own behavior and his belief structures. Later in life he wrote that the CEO's main job is to constantly rethink everything.[23] That is what he did.

The changes at Semco took time. Semler was carving new space and learning as he went. Today, he makes no decisions; in fact, he has not made a decision for Semco in about 20 years. The employees make all the decisions.

The decision-making started with the dress code, then the hours workers would keep, then the color, layout, and design of the workspace. Today, all decisions at Semco are made by the employees, including the amount of their own salaries, how they divide the share of the profit they earn, what new products they will build, and what companies they will acquire. He didn't believed that his employees wanted to drag themselves to work, or escape early, or do

22 Ricardo Semler, Maverick: the Success Story Behind the World's Most Unusual Workplace, Warner Books, New York, p.58
23 Ricardo Semler, The Seven-Day Weekend: Changing the Way Work Works, Penguin Group, USA, p.183

as little as they could possibly get away with while pushing their union for the most pay they could finagle out of Semco. He saw these people as capable parents raising children, attending PTA meetings, electing lawmakers, and felt that at Semco they should be treated as adults.[24]

Semler believes the unions play an important role, and he encourages workers to unionize. Unions provide protection for workers. While Semco doesn't always get along with its unions it enables its employees to unionize and provides organizers protection against persecution by others in the company.[25]

Semco operates based on a team approach. Major decisions are team-based. One day Semler had a brainstorm that his team could build a consumer version of a commercial dishwasher that could wash dishes in 90 seconds. He called a meeting to discuss his idea, and not one person showed up. No one in the company shared his enthusiasm for the idea he thought was ingenious, so it wasn't pursued.

A few months later, a competitor came out with a very similar machine. Semler wanted to throw it back in the faces of all the employees who didn't show up to his meeting. However, eighteen months later the competitor gave up on the dishwasher. Semler realized that being the

---

24 Semler, Ricardo. Maverick: The Success Story behind the World's Most Unusual Workplace. New York, NY: Warner, 1993. P. 59

25 Peter A. Maresco, Christopher C. York, Ricardo Semler: Creating Organizational Change Through Employee Empowered, https://www.google.com/url?sa=t&rct=j&q=&esrc=s&source=web&cd=1&ved=0CD AQFjAA&url=http%3A%2F%2Fwww.researchgate.net%2Fpublictopics. PublicPostFileLoader.html%3Fid%3D542a20b9d2fd6454198b4567%26key %3D2f5fbb92-e1a2-4905-a18c-c29727fad021&ei=eh1rVaH5LMvVoASTz4 G4CQ&usg=AFQjCNF0cBeVa094skzW_soYiWeiPGidlg&sig2=D4X5kC1 c9AWaia79jcPX9w&bvm=bv.94455598,d.cGU Accessed 31 May 2015

owner of the company doesn't mean that every idea he thinks has merit actually does.

Semler says that for a company to be its best, employees first priority is their own self-interest. It is not the company's interest that is the worker's foremost priority. He believes an employee who puts himself or herself first will be more motivated to perform well.[26] As part of leveraging that self-interest ,Ricardo Semler initiated a profit sharing plan. We will see a bit later in this book that one of the things that distinguishes the best companies is that they have a profit sharing plan. Semler points out, "What is an annual bonus, after all, but a form of profit sharing." He goes onto point out that a poorly designed profit sharing plan can produced resentment and division. He doesn't use an annual bonus structure. If you want a great 20 minute investment in learning something useful about profit-sharing, read Chapter 17 in Semler's book Maverick. Aligning an employee's interest and passions with the work that employee does is the only true way to let people perform their best.

Parents know this is true. Parents are always trying to get their children to work hard and do well in school. When our daughter was in sixth grade, she announced that she wanted to go to an exclusive all-girls college prep high school. She was a hard worker, but was a middle-of-the-pack student, and each year this high school only took the top girls from my daughter's grade school. We were supportive and said, "Sure. However, they are quite selective." It turned out this was something our daughter really wanted. You can guess how well she did in seventh

26 Semler, Ricardo. The Seven-day Weekend: Changing the Way Work Works. New York: Portfolio, 2004. P. 41

and eighth grades and which high school she went to.

Self-interest is a powerful motivator.

How has Semco done? The biggest test for any company is how it fares during a recession. Through the worst decade-long recession in Brazil's history, the top line grew 600%, profits were up 500%, and worker productivity rose 700%. From a single $4 million company in 1980 Semco has grown into several wholly-owned companies generating over one billion dollars in revenue[27] plus a minority share investment in other companies that add up to $9 billion in market value.[28]

Semler's company is always trying new things. He says he is guided by six principles[29]:

1. Don't increase business size unnecessarily.
2. Never stop being a start-up.
3. Don't be a nanny to your workers.
4. Let talent find its place.
5. Make decisions quickly and openly.
6. Partner promiscuously. You can't do it all yourself.

Most management techniques employed in companies today were informed by how our parents managed us as children. "I'm your parent, and you will do as you're

27 Blakeman, Chuck. "Why 'Participation Age' Leaders Will Beat Old-School Managers, Every Time." Inc.com. N.p., n.d. Web. 31 Jan. 2015. <http://www.inc.com/chuck-blakeman/marissa-mayer-the-old-school-manager-vs-ricardo-semler-the-participation-age-lea.html>.
28 "Ricardo Semler Started by Herman @ Live on Demand." YouTube. YouTube, n.d. Web. 31 Jan. 2015. <https://www.youtube.com/watch?v=1wk9ryFuTwo>.
29 Ibid

told!" Semler points out that because command and control management techniques appear to work well most managers don't stop to think about how negatively such military-inspired policies impact people. He says rather than being truly effective, such strategies are usually destructive.[30]

Semco has successfully followed Semler's model for decades. And like the turn-around at Harley Davidson, and the long successful run that Motorola enjoyed under Galvin, and the on-going success at Toyota, Semco's performance has been nothing short of phenomenal. They all use a leadership style that makes those at the top less and less critical to the development of strategy and even less critical to the operation of the company. Why haven't many more companies adopted this approach? How do you change the thinking at the top of the company?

It is a puzzle. When faced with overwhelming evidence on what makes a company extraordinarily successful, why do managers find it very difficult to confront their own habits and behaviors even when that's what the CEO wants? The approach is usually to define core values and expect the right behaviors to follow.[31] The next story hints at an approach that gets these kinds of results quickly

---

30 Semler, Ricardo. The Seven-day Weekend: Changing the Way Work Works. New York: Portfolio, 2004. P 165
31 People have said this so often that most leaders believe its true: values drive behavior. Psychologists have repeatedly demonstrated, starting with the dramatic experiment by Stanley Milgram, that values have much less influence on behavior than does the socialized environment.

"**A**head two-thirds!" U.S. Navy Captain David Marquet ordered his senior Officer of the Deck, Lieutenant Commander Bill Green.

"Ahead two-thirds!" repeated the Santa Fe's OOD.

The Captain expected to feel the boat surge ahead. Nothing happened. The helmsman did not carry out the order. Marquet peered around the periscope tube. The helmsman was squirming in his chair. The captain asked him what was going on.

"Captain, there is no ahead two-thirds on the EPM," replied the helmsman. On every other submarine Marquet had served on the Electric Propulsion Motor (EPM) had an "ahead two-thirds." Marquet hadn't known that there was only an "ahead one-third" on the Santa Fe's EPM.

After years serving on various submarines, the Santa Fe was Marquet's first command. It was not the boat he had prepared for. Originally, he was to be assigned to the nuclear submarine Olympia. He trained for a year and studied every aspect of that ship, from design and engineering to maintenance reports to crew evaluations and every problem the ship had ever encountered. He knew that ship well and was ready to take command. However, at the last moment Marquet was vectored to a different vessel, the newer submarine, the USS Santa Fe. His knowledge of the Olympia would be useless on the Santa Fe.

While the Olympia was in tip-top shape, with high crew retention and above-average inspection scores, the Santa Fe was a troubled boat. It had the worst retention numbers in the entire submarine force and was the boat that everyone joked about. Captain Marquet's boss gave him carte blanche to "change out people" on the sub. Since he did not know them and none had had the benefit of his leadership, he elected to keep this 'worst' crew intact.

When Marquet realized the he had just given an order that could not be executed by the helmsman, he called over the OOD who had repeated the order. Did the OOD know that there was no 'ahead two-thirds' on the EPM, the captain wanted to know.

"Yes, Captain, I did."

"Well why did you order it?"

"Because you told me to."[32]

This was a wake-up call for Marquet. In that moment

---

[32] Marquet, L. David. Turn the Ship Around!: A True Story of Turning Followers into Leaders. New York: Portfolio, 2012. P..86

Captain Marquet realized that the Santa Fe had a captain who'd trained for a different boat, and a crew inclined to follow whatever orders were given. On a submarine this was a deadly combination and needed to be fixed quickly.[33]

Marquet needed to change how the boat operated. He needed a change in thinking and a change in behavior. However, changing how people think runs smack into the obstacle that behavioral economists like Nobel laureate Daniel Kahneman have been researching: that it actually can take a long time for people to change their thinking, particularly if it requires them to abandon long-held habits. This isn't willful stubbornness, it is how our brains work.

Marquet needed the change to happen in three days!

Marquet solved this problem in a very insightful way. He realized he did not have time to change the thinking. Instead, he recognized that all he really wanted was a change in behavior. He realized that all you get from people is their behavior. That you don't actually know what they are thinking, nor do you need to know what they are thinking as long as you get the behavior you are after. This proved to be a powerful insight.

As a commander, all you have to do to get a change in behavior is ask for the change in behavior. You must be specific. And when you are, the behavior is observable, and people can readily give you that behavior change. You can get the behavior you want, even without agreement on the reasons behind the change in behavior. It worked on

33 "How Great Leaders Serve Others: David Marquet at TEDxScottAFB." YouTube. N.p., n.d. Web. 01 Feb. 2015. <http://youtu.be/ DLRH5J_93LQ>. Min. 7:30

the Santa Fe. In the end, Marquet believed that most of the crew eventually changed their thinking once they changed their behavior. But, if they didn't, it didn't matter that much to Captain Marquet. After all, they were delivering the behavior as if they believed in the change.

To keep his lack of knowledge of the ship and his crew's habit of compliance from killing all of them, Marquet enacted a change in how people handled their jobs. He decided he was not going to give any orders. Instead of waiting to be ordered to do something, the crew member who was responsible for performing the task would say, "I intend to..." For example, "Captain, I intend to dive the boat!" To which Marquet might ask a question or two like, "Is the crew below deck?" and, "Are the hatches closed and locked?" Once Marquet had the information he needed, he would say, "Very well." He started with his senior officers first, but eventually used the technique in dealing with all crew members.

After a while, Marquet realized that he should not have to ask questions like, "Is the crew below deck?" or, "Are the hatches closed and locked?" or, "What's the depth beneath the boat?" One day, when his OOD said, "I intend to submerge," Marquet asked him what questions the OOD thought Marquet might be thinking about. Of course, the OOD could anticipate every question the captain might ask.

From that point forward, crew members gave their thought process and rationale for the intended action. The crew member might say something like, "I intend to submerge. The depth is 400 feet. Crew is below, hatches sealed, the boat is trimmed for dive." And so on.

This caused each person on the crew to think like the person senior to him. In the long run, this thinking-like-the-boss mentality had an interesting outcome. Over the following years, a disproportionate number of promotions had been issued to Santa Fe officers[34] and crew since adopting the "I intend to..." model.

By putting the initiative into the hands of the doers, Marquet changed the responsibility from the boss to the worker. Along with the ownership of the action went the pride in doing a job well. The mantra on the Santa Fe went from "I do what I'm told to do," to "I do what I should do. Nobody needs to tell me what to do. I know my job better than anyone."

Think about your own company and its workforce. If that statement isn't true for all your employees right now, then you have a great opportunity.

The transformation on the Santa Fe did not happen overnight, but eventually the whole ship and every crew member operated under the "I intend to..." model. In the end, the crew, with support of the officers, ignored old doctrine in favor of better ways to get the job done, and by doing so, changed some Navy procedures. By the end of the first year, the Santa Fe had gone from worst submarine in the U.S. Navy's fleet to the best. Keep in mind that this performance and the subsequent phenomenal promotion rate came from the 'worst' crew that Captain Marquet had inherited. This is a key lesson. In the business world, we have lots of stories where a leader came in and turned

---

34 Both Executive Officers and all four department heads have since achieved the rank of Captain. This is extraordinarily unusual in the Navy.

around the situation keeping the same people in place. It's about the environment the leader creates, rather than 'right people' and it is never personal charisma. Recall that Robert Galvin asked, "They're all good people, how do we make them great?" That is the CEO's most important job.

Earlier we mentioned profit sharing, but how do you do profit sharing on a nuclear submarine? Obviously, that's impossible to do, there is no profit. However, as a good stand-in, Marquet knew they would sail into a combat zone and scheduled the reenlistment ceremony while there. Reenlistment bonuses paid in a combat zone are tax free. In that first year Captain Marquet awarded over half a million dollars in reenlistment bonuses to 36 sailors (that was 12 times the number of reenlistment in the prior year).

The final company we are taking a look at had an unlikely start. It began operations in 1990, in a mature industry, with lots of smart competitors serving a handful of large, dominant customers. This market hardly looked like a place of great opportunity. Yet this company jumped into this challenging environment and has grown rapidly. Today it is the biggest player in its market. It is a highly profitable, innovative company with an extraordinarily productive workforce. In an industry that grows at a just one percent per year, this company has enjoyed double digit growth every year for the past 20 years.[35] Today, The Morning Star Packing Company supplies 40% of the U.S. ingredient tomato paste and diced tomato markets.[36]

---

35 http://www.managementexchange.com/blog/when-nobody-and-everybody-boss?utm_source=MIX+Fix&utm_campaign=db6d9181c0-The_MIX_Fix_Mar_09_2012&utm_medium=email accessed July 6th 2014
36 "Company History." Morning Star :::. N.p., n.d. Web. 04 Feb. 2015. <http://morningstarco.com/index.cgi?Page=About+Us%2FCompany+History>.

In 1970, Chris Rufer, an MBA student in southern California, started a trucking company that hauled tomatoes from the field to the processing plant. Starting a trucking company was a lucky beginning for Rufer because it exposed him to an interesting management insight that informed how he organized his later ventures. He asked himself, 'how can you manage truck drivers?' You can put a supervisor in every truck, but that did not seem sensible, who manages the supervisors? Rufer realized that all truck drivers have to be capable of managing themselves.[37]

In 1990, Rufer formed The Morning Star Packing Company, which processed tomatoes in a facility in Los Banos, California.[38] His vision was to create an organization that enabled top performance among employees. [39]

What Rufer stumbled upon was the same thing that Ricardo Semler realized: you can organize a company such that the management structure is superfluous. And when you do, the performance of the team skyrockets. Rufer had one advantage over Semler: he initiated his management philosophy as he started his company. Semler had to change management philosophy in a going concern. That required lots of changes in thinking and took Semler years to fully implement.

In looking at Morning Star, the Harvard Business Review

---

37 Buchanan, Leigh. "One Company's Audacious Org Chart: 400 Leaders, 0 Bosses." Inc. Magazine. Inc., 18 Apr. 2013. Web. 4 Feb. 2015. <http%3A%2F%2Fwww.inc.com%2Faudacious-companies%2Fleigh-buchanan%2Fmorning-star.html>.
38 According to Wikipedia, "The name Los Banos is Spanish for "the baths", and was originally spelled Los Baños. Its official spelling is without the eñe,
39 In 1995 Morning Star added a second facility and a third in 2002.

noted, that the ratio of manager to employees in a small organization may have one manager for 10 employees. Thus, if you had 100,000 frontline employees you'd need 10,000 manager, then another 1,000 to manage them, and 100 for that next level, then 10 and finally one manager for a total of 11,111 managers. If managers on average earn three times as much as the average frontline employee then management costs would add one third to the salary line. Management is expensive.[40]

Rufer's insight from working with truck drivers allowed him to successfully challenge the most fundamental dogma of management: that management hierarchy gives you control, and without it you have chaos. What Rufer has successfully shown, as have Ricardo Semler and Captain Marquet, is that you get more control without the hierarchy and you get far better performance. Hierarchy implies a parent-to-child relationship. Adults hate being forced into the child position.

At Morning Star everyone is an adult and a manager—a manager of themselves and their team. However, the organization runs with no bosses, nobody in the 'parent' role. There is plenty of structure and a strong culture of accountability. Every employee enters into an agreement called a CLOU (Colleague Letter of Understanding) in which each colleague describes their personal commercial mission, their responsibilities and activities, and their personal development goals.

The way Morning Star employees handle the personal

40 Hamel, Gary. "First, Let's Fire All the Managers." Harvard Business Review. Harvard Business Review, 01 Dec. 2011. Web. Accessed 03 Feb. 2015. <https://hbr.org/2011/12/first-lets-fire-all-the-managers>.

commercial mission is telling. One job in the tomato processing plant is to stand alongside a conveyer of tomatoes as they come off the trucks and pick out debris and bad tomatoes. The job description might read, "Your job is to remove debris, foreign material, and bad tomatoes as they pass you on the conveyor belt." However, at Morning Star the personal commercial mission the colleague writes for himself or herself would more likely read, "My mission is to ensure our customers receive pristine tomato products free of foreign material." This mission gives the work a much higher degree of importance. If this job is not done well, then nothing that anyone else in the plant does will overcome the impact of low quality on the customer.

In the beginning of this monograph, we talked about creating and sustaining competitive advantage. One problem that needs to be solved constantly is, "How do we have the strongest possible relationship with the customer?" Morning Star's personal commercial missions are a perfect response to that problem.

This level of autonomy is not for every worker, but those who don't fit in easily self-select out of the company within a year or two. For those who do fit, Morning Star is a great place to work.

Insight

What is remarkable about the environments these highly successful organizations create is that they do not emphasize the kinds of initiatives often suggested as ways to engage employees. Their successes stem from letting people contribute as smart, thoughtful, responsible adults. It isn't about providing the traditional top-down engagement strategies such as articulating and sharing the leader's vision; defining the company's core values and using them to hire and fire; sponsoring well intentioned programs such as restaurant vouchers, healthy food options, and gym memberships; fostering social interactions with meal sharing; giving staff access to cultural events; or any of hundreds of other similar tactics decided and delivered from the top. And trying them over and over again.

There is one thing wrong with such strategies. They do not lift employee engagement nearly as much as they are designed to. Studies done by firms specializing in employee engagement show a consistent level of low employee engagement year-in-and-year-out. Albert Einstein once said, "The definition of insanity is doing the same thing over and over and expecting different results." This

39

implies that we should examine the effectiveness of a strategy before repeating it. And the data is conclusive: these activities fail to generate the desired results.

The ultra successful organizations we've looked at do not subscribe to such top-down, command and control approaches. With top-down approaches, companies create parent-to-child structures. If you continuously put adults into child roles, in many subtle ways, childish behavior is what you will get. Your people will come up to (or down to) the maturity level your set for them, determined by how you speak to them. The value of adult employees is their adult minds. It is from those adult minds that companies find great solutions to the ongoing competitive problems we listed earlier:

- How do we maintain the strongest possible relationship with the customer?
- How do we package?
- How do we market?
- How do we price?
- How do we sell?
- How do we service?
- How do we get the customer to feel kinship with us through our solution?
- How do we give the customer identity through our solution?
- How do we create meaning for the customer through our solution?

Throughout 2013, Inc. magazine's economist-in-residence, Gary Kunkle, conducted a research study of more than 100,000 U.S.-based midsize businesses (those with 85 to 999 employees). Kunkle wanted to identify companies that are sustained-growth champions; that is, those that added head count for five consecutive years. What is key is the time period studied, 2007 to 2012. This included the Great Recession of 2007 to 2009. If a company was growing steadily even during a time of economic downturn, it made the cut. Only 1.5% of companies made the cut. The study then dug into a sample of 100 companies (the Build 100) in this top group.

These top 100 companies in the survey had little in common. They were not concentrated into special geographies, or predicable industry clusters. They had varied customer bases and were as likely to be relatively new entities as long-established firms.

Two big finding bind these top companies together. First, the leadership in these companies attributed growth to the company's cultural environment, (how they work as a team to resolve issues, how they treat customers, and how they interact together) rather than other factors like financing or product design. Second, when you share the wealth created, you get higher performance and better talent retention. How you treat your employees is paramount, and sharing financial success with employees aligns them to an outcome that drives productivity and higher revenue growth.[41]

The Brazilian company Semco, for example, allocates 23% of after-tax profit as the employees' share of income. The workers in each business unit meet and decide—by simple majority vote—what they want to do with it. In most units, that has turned out to be an equal distribution to employees. The guy who sweeps the floor gets just as much as a division leader.

Like Semco, the organizations we've looked at here are not companies where you see a burst of growth followed by a lull, then renewed growth and another lull. Kunkle's organizations delivered steady, predictable growth that surpassed all their competitors. They aren't the ones chasing the competition; they've <u>become the competition</u>. These companies are the hare with the work ethic of the tortoise. They get 90% of their ideas and innovations from individual employees.

Kunkle's study also revealed that the best performing

---

41 Leibs, Scott. "Grow. Hire. Repeat." Inc. Magazine. Inc., 25 Feb. 2014. Web. 6 Feb. 2015. <http://www.inc.com/magazine/201403/scott-leibs/sustained-growth-predicts-business-success.html>.

companies share a common worry with almost all small and mid-sized enterprises: they feel least confident of their sales ability. The better a company gets at solving our list of competeability problems, the easier the sales job becomes, and the more confident the company will be when it comes to sales.

All of the organizations we've looked at have been well publicized. Books have been written about most of them. The question you have to ask is, "With so much evidence for the success of these companies, why is their success so difficult to mimic?"

Leaders in companies find it nearly impossible to mimic the success of the companies discussed here and those in Kunkle's study for three reasons.

First, until recently we did not have a roadmap and a set of tried-and-true tools to allow a company to systematically move into this space. Today that roadmap and tool-kit exists.

Second, managers are not specific about what behavior drives success. The common wisdom suggests that values drive behavior. Get the values right and the right behavior will follow. This is not correct.

That doesn't stop leaders from establishing a mission and a set of values to drive that mission, and a vision of what the next end-state for the company looks like, and expecting that the values will drive behavior and the mission will guide the work in the direction of the vision. We can point to volumes of research that shows a much stronger determinant of behavior is the social norm. Plus,

43

Captain Marquet showed us that you can get the behavior you want simply by asking for it. Values don't do that. (If you're interested in the topic of values and behavior, read the first chapter of *Behave! How to get 100% of your workers fully engaged*.)

Third, and more important, theories and the habits around the way the company operates are huge obstacles.

Ten years after publishing the Blue Ocean Strategy, which recommends that companies can create a leap in value by creating 'blue oceans' of uncontested market space, the authors, W. Chan Kim and Renée Mauborgne, revisited why so many companies struggle to do so. In conversations with many managers tasked with creating market making strategies they found that the one common reality which routinely undermined their efforts to change, were their pre-existing mind sets. Their ingrained assumptions and adopted theories about how the existing business works prevented them from being able to create new uncontested market spaces.[42]

Nobel Prize laureate Daniel Kahneman states that this phenomenon is a function of how our brains work. Once you have accepted a practice it becomes a tool in your thinking. It then become extremely difficult to perceive its flaws. When you run into information that does not seem to conform to the model you've adopted you assume there is some good explanation that you're just missing.[43]

---

42 W. Chan Kim & Renée Mauborgne, "Red Ocean Traps." Harvard Business Review. N.p., 01 Mar. 2015. Web. 08 Mar. 2015. <https://hbr.org/2015/03/red-ocean-traps#>.
43 Kahneman, Daniel. Thinking, Fast and Slow. New York: Farrar, Straus and Giroux, 2011. p.277

Einstein also said, "It is the theory which decides what we can observe."[44]

For example, in a global meeting of economists, one of their members, Maurice Allais, devised a choice experiment that they all participated in. What they did not realize was that the choices they made in the experiment proved that a theory they all loved was wrong. Allais revealed this bombshell at the end of the meeting, and anticipated that the economists would be immediately convinced to give up the theory and adopt one that better described the real outcome. Even this most powerful and personal demonstration of the data failed to unseat the theory.

The economists (including several who would later win Nobel Prizes) stubbornly continued to use the faulty theory as part of their economic tool kits despite its flaw.

The point is, here we have a bunch of scientists whose life work is the search for truth, finding themselves hamstrung by a quirk of human psychology called Theory Induced Blindness, a term coined by Daniel Kahneman.[45]

This problem affects everyone. Daniel Kahneman points out that we have a very difficult time abandoning deeply entrenched belief structures. It is almost insurmountable to accomplish a change of this scale by first thinking it through, and then acting.

When Kahneman was a young man, he personally

44 Heisenberg, Werner. Physics and Beyond; Encounters and Conversations. New York: Harper & Row, 1971. p. 63

45 Kahneman, Daniel. Thinking, Fast and Slow. New York: Farrar, Straus and Giroux, 2011. P.277

experienced the power of an entrenched belief. In his case, it was his belief in his ability to observe and evaluate the behavior of others. As a soldier assigned to the Israeli Army Psychology Branch, Kahneman was tasked with evaluating candidates for officer training. His job was to observe behavior of the candidates facing a challenge and, based on that behavior, determine how the candidate would do in officer training. The Israeli Army was looking for things like natural leadership ability, teamwork skills, problem solving skill, resilience, etc.

The challenge was one the Israeli Army had borrowed from the British Army. Teams of candidates who didn't know one another, with no rank or name on their uniforms, were tasked with lifting a log over a six-foot high wall and getting all the soldiers over the wall while not allowing the log or the soldiers to touch the wall. It is a difficult challenge and no team gets it right the first time.

Kahneman and a colleague would observe the interaction of the soldiers, seeing who stepped up to lead, who was the aggressive problem solver, who was the thinker, who played well with others and who didn't, and who pouted when their idea was rejected. They would then collaborate and make predictions on how the candidates would perform in these areas in officer training. Every few weeks they would get a new group to evaluate and over time, Kahneman and his colleague became very confident in their ability to make accurate predictions.

Months later, Kahneman and his colleague would get reports on how the candidates actually performed during officer training. Their predictions were no better than they would have been had they just flipped a coin. Their ability to predict accurately was a complete fiction. However, as Kahneman humorously pointed out, the fact that the whole process had no value did not influence the Army; they kept repeating the log-over-the-wall exercise anyway.

What Kahneman found most interesting in all this was that despite his training as a psychologist and his knowledge that he and his colleague never accurately predicted training outcomes, each time they evaluated a new set of candidates they felt absolutely confident that <u>this time</u> they would get it right. They never did. We all share this unbounded capacity to delude ourselves confidently.

Changing how leaders interact with other workers involves just such an obstacle of ingrained behaviors and beliefs.

In running companies, leaders take actions that feel like the right actions. When we think we're doing the right thing, our brain creates an emotional bond to that behavior. Our existing success model inhibits our ability to make the emotional decision that the evidence and the rational argument call for. We are stuck with our frame of reference and it is very difficult to consider a different model.

For many businesses, the leader's frame-of-reference is very narrow. You can only see how successful you are, <u>not</u> how successful you could have been. Just as Ricardo Semler pointed out, Captain Marquet also realized that the apparent success of a top-down leadership model makes it easy to rationalize.[46] But, its apparent success is over the short term. In the Navy, when the performance of a team deteriorates after an officer departs, then the belief is that

46 Marquet, L. David. Turn the Ship Around!: A True Story of Turning Followers into Leaders. New York: Portfolio, 2012. P. 24

he or she was a good leader, rather than suspecting that the officer failed to properly train the crew.[47] When Marquet left the Santa Fe, its terrific performance continued because it was a result of the whole crew's performance, not dependent upon any single individual and certainly not on Marquet.

After Ricardo Semler had his health scare, he decided overnight to change the way he led his company. Figuring out how required a lot more changes in his thinking. It took Semler many small incremental and experimental steps over the course of twenty years to get to the point where Semco runs so well.

Marquet solved the fundamental problem of his narrow frame of reference on the Santa Fe by ignoring the thinking and going straight to the behavior. But his changes in a tight closed environment still took months to take hold. You can use techniques that combine the learning from Semco, Marquet and The Morning Star Company to make the process faster and surer. The trick is to modify behavior and not worry too much about the thinking, even your own thinking. It will eventually follow along. The Manufacturing P.A.R. Excellence (ParX) process contains a set of tried and true tools and techniques which compress what took Semler and Morning Star years to figure out, into a few months of programmed step-by-step implementation. Significant change is never easy, but a well defined roadmap makes it easier.

---

47 Ibid. P.25

A t Harley Davidson their interpretation of having employees with a deep sense of ownership was something they called EI or Employee Involvement. It was something they borrowed from the Japanese.

Harley's CEO Rich Teerlink said, "True employee involvement is a process by which you actually run the business. It means pushing management responsibility down as far as possible. It means that the employee accepts the responsibility for saying, 'If there is something that can help me do my job better or make a higher quality product then I'm going to do it, or tell someone else in the company about it.' That's employee involvement"

Harley's single most important insight, and one that had been virtually ignored by U.S. industry, was something W. Edward Deming taught. "If you get past his (Deming's) angry crotchety approach to American management, you realize he has the right idea. He's saying, 'Hey, management,

49

you have to change and you have to provide tools to your people so they can change…leadership should come from the people." According to Ron Hutchinson, Harley's management chieftain supporting the remarkable quality changes the employees delivered.[48]

Every good CEO knows that the best way to change anything is to follow a defined process. Map out the change you need, and follow that map. However, before you can develop the roadmap, you must have a deep understanding of exactly where you want to end up and how you get there.

Where you want to end up is crystal clear. All the organizations we looked at, along with the findings in the lean production study, ended up pointing to how you deal with people. Success is achieved when you create a sustained sense of ownership in the people. It is that sense of ownership that drives people to care, to innovate, and to embrace a feeling of pride in a job well done. You will create more wealth for yourself, your employees, and your community when you run a company where your people share a robust sense of ownership in the company. The amount of data and studies supporting this is staggering. Companies who do this typically show twice the rate of productivity improvement, twice the level of customer loyalty, grow profits as much as three times faster, and have employee turnover 87 percent lower than companies where the employees have no sense of ownership[49]. This is where you want to go.

48 Reid, Peter C. Well Made in America: Lessons from Harley-Davidson on Being the Best. New York: McGraw-Hill, 1990. P 73, 79
49 Show Me the Money: The ROI of Employee Engagement,Reese Haydon, https://www.decision-wise.com/show-me-the-money-the-roi-of-employee-engagement/, accessed 3/29/2017

It's the 'how to get there' where the problem hides. As we saw with the companies we looked at, their 'how to get there' was not immediately clear. For each of them it took years of experimentation to find the formula that worked for them. It is the work I undertook five years ago and I am still honing to this day.

You may be thinking what Ralph Stayer, owner of Johnsonville Foods, used to say to himself before he made the right changes and the company began to grow. "I can't expect them (employees) to be as committed to the company as I am. After all, I own the place. They don't." Stayer went on to point out that most of his peers felt the same way. Eventually he proved himself wrong.

This book is my fourth. In all my work, I look for tools that pass two rigorous tests. First, the solution must be tried-and-true. Hundreds of companies or thousands of people must have used it successfully. Second, the solution must be supported by science. In most cases, since we are dealing with people's behavior the science comes from psychology or behavioral economics.

It is a tactical choice to describe your destination as 'a sense of ownership' rather than 'employee engagement'. The benefit of this approach is that it opens up our strategy to broader research since a sense of ownership can occur in areas other than business. We have a sense of ownership over things we own, our ideas, our favorite sports team, our pets, and even our families. Through this enlarged filter we can look for findings in studies centered around the creation of a sense of ownership That enables us to understand the prerequisites needed to achieve that

51

same sense of ownership in our people for their work and workplace.

These studies reveal some interesting truths around what drives a sense of ownership. First, there are the conditions that we need to meet in order for this sense of ownership to flourish. Second, there are strong motivators that drive the desired behaviors of high productivity and problem-solving that we need to create.

The conditions that need to exist include employees feeling a high level of autonomy and control. They must have the ability to be effective in their work. They also must feel licensed to take an idea forward without having to deal with unwarranted, unnecessary and bureaucratic obstacles. Finally, they must be able to develop strong sense personal belonging with co-workers. In the lean manufacturing studies, these are the conditions that drive the 'production management policy', and in Kunkle's study, these are the elements of a 'company's cultural environment' which cause these companies to have such extraordinary results.

The strong motivators in these high competeability companies are also different. The traditional 'Pain, Fear and Gain' are powerful and effective motivators and form the backbone of a command-and-control management environment. However, they are not the backbone motivators in high competeability companies. Pain, Fear, and Gain motivators suffer from two problems. First they are negative. Pain and Fear are obviously viewed negatively by the person experiencing them; Gain is negative in that it appeals to our sense of greed, which is generally consider a negative force. When applied, they often put an adult in the child role, which is damaging to their sense of identity. Second they are short-term drivers. When the fear is gone, so is the motivator. The same is true with Pain and Gain. These three motivators are hard to eliminate completely. Nevertheless we strive to minimize them in a peer-to-peer

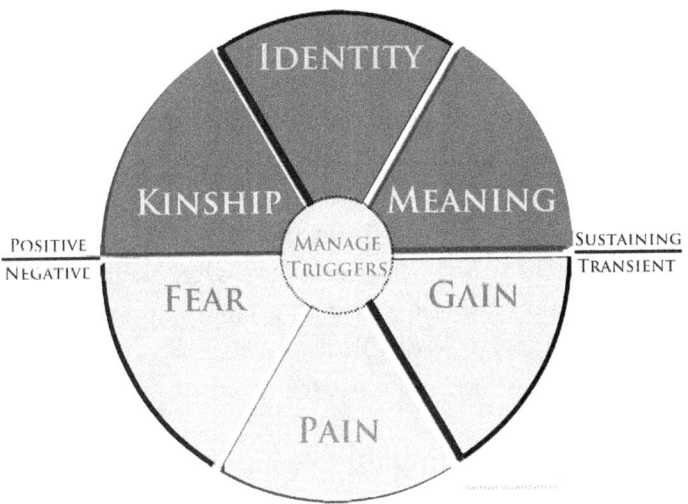

accountability model.

There are three distinct motivational drivers identified in

the studies around employee sense of ownership[50]. First is kinship. This is the condition of feeling personal belonging. It is about having an environment that encourages people to develop strong friendships at work. In their 2017 report State of the American Workplace, Gallup reports[51],

"The best friend question sometimes gets a bad rap, but it consistently shows a strong relationship to improvements in customer engagement, profit, employee safety incidents and patient safety incidents…friendships can take on a very powerful dynamic in which casual, friendly conversations turn into innovative discussions"

In high competeability companies, employees have friends. Kinship is a powerful motivator for a sense of ownership.

Second is identity. Identity is how we see ourselves and how others see us. We work hard to establish the right identity. We'll have one identity at work, a different one in our immediate family, a slightly different one in our extended family, and perhaps a completely different identity when we go out for a beer with our college buddies. Each of these distinct identities is important to us. There is a strong correlation between achieving a sense of ownership and the ability to establish and maintain a desired identity at work. To the extent that we can foster that identity, we promote a sense of ownership.

Third is meaning. Creating meaning in the work we do

---

50 Ozler, Hayrettin, Abdullah Yilmaz, and Derya Ozler. "Psychological Ownership: An Empirical Study on Its Antecedents and Impacts upon Organizational Behaviors." Problems and Perspectives in Management 6.3 (2008): 38-47. Web. 3 Apr. 2017. <https://businessperspectives.org/journals_free/ppm/2008/PPM_EN_2008_03_Ozler.pdf>

51 State of the American Workplace, 2017 Gallup, Inc. Accessed April 2, 2017 http://www.gallup.com/reports/199961/state-american-workplace-report-2017.aspx

enables us to take ownership of the behavior we're responsible for and the outcomes that behavior creates. (It enhances our ability to create identity too.) Meaning is personal. It doesn't matter if the people around you don't get the same meaning from the same work. As long as you can create the meaning you want to see, you are motivated.

Kinship, Identity, and Meaning are different from Pain, Fear, and Gain in two ways. First, they are very positive motivators. Second, they tend to sustain and are more resilient than Pain, Fear, and Gain.

Thus, we need to find the right tools that allow the company to deliver that high level of autonomy coupled with the key motivators of Kinship, Identity, and Meaning.

A utonomy is giving up total control at the top. The trouble is you cannot just give control to everyone else. They have to take control. Before they will take control they have to want to take control and see it as serving their best interest. Thus, you cannot give up control without making sure someone else takes control. To make that happen you need a strong accountability structure along with the accurate and timely measurements. The good news is that it doesn't take much to get people to want autonomy.

In addition, you want to put process around accountability and rhythm around measurement such that you're sure nothing slips through the cracks. Control is a disciplined activity.

Since being able to get stuff done is crucial to building a sense of ownership, you want to make sure you have the right seats, and the right people in those seats.

Then you want to be deliberate with your motivation efforts around Kinship, Identity, and Meaning. To the extent that you can influence those motivators, you will put in place tools to let them do their magic. Motivators that leverage Pain, Fear, and Gain actually undermine a sense of ownership except in certain circumstances. Generally, you're better off keeping them out of your motivation tactics.

Finally, you need a very good problem solving methodology that everyone utilizes, along with a defined innovation path that takes risk out of the equation (which sound impossible, but with a little creativity, we can do it).
The commercial entities we've talked about here have been manufacturers, Harley Davidson, Toyota, Morning Star Company, Motorola and Semco. The only exception was U.S.S. Santa Fe. The submarine story was included because it pointed to the insight on focusing on behavior rather than thinking. Behavior is key because it is the observable performance you get from employees. You cannot see what they are thinking.

We did not deliberately pick manufacturers. However, manufacturers face a different management challenge than do service companies and have a deeper need for getting their employees to have a sense of ownership. As a consequence, when we went looking for a tool-kit, we wanted one that would work for manufacturers.

Many manufacturers must manage all the same things that a typical service company must manage. That includes Finance, Sales and Marketing, Customer Service, IT, HR and so on. On top of those functions, manufacturers have a set of complex activities to manage and coordinate that typical service companies do not. They include: Purchasing and Supply Chain, Production, Maintenance, Logistics, a complex Regulatory environment, Advanced Manufacturing Technology, Capital Equipment Planning, Engineering, Design, and Quality Control. One of the two key differences between running a manufacturing company and a service company is the sheer number of difficult manufacturing problems that come up every minute. The manufacturing team develops 'Band-Aid' habits to resolve problems quickly. Running a manufacturing company is more complex and demanding than running a service company. I know there will be service company executives that will bristle at that statement, and perhaps for their specific companies this difference does not hold. However, it does hold true at the broad industry level.

The other key difference has to do with innovation.

Data shows that service companies derive most of their innovative ideas from customers and manifest those ideas in organizational changes. Manufacturers, on the other hand, source most of their innovative ideas from employees, and these ideas mostly turn into product and process changes. If you are depending upon your employees to generate the bulk of your innovations and thus your competeability, then you want them to be motivated and able to provide those innovations. Of course there are service industries where the creative output of employees is critical to creating competitive advantage and those particular service industries would be wise to consider following a path closer to one designed for manufacturers.

Even more interesting is the data from the Build 100

companies in the Kunkle study mentioned earlier[52]. Most of the companies in the Build 100 are service companies[53]. These are highly competitive companies where 90% of their best ideas come from individual employees are unlike average service companies where the bulk of ideas come from customers.

Thus, even in non-manufacturing companies, putting your people in the position of producing great innovative ideas is key to creating and sustaining competitive advantage.

---

52 Leibs, Scott. "What Inspires (And Worries) The Build 100." Inc. com. Inc., 26 Feb. 2014. Web. 09 Apr. 2017. <https://www.inc.com/magazine/201403/sustained-growth-dna-business-strengths.html>.
53 "The Build 100 List of Sustained-Growth Companies." Inc.com. Inc., 26 Feb. 2014. Web. 09 Apr. 2017. <https://www.inc.com/build100>.

Thinking Slow

Innovation is simply a form of problem-solving. If you want your company to be truly competitive, then your people must be good problem-solvers. It helps to understand the following about problem solving:

There are three levels of problem-solving, and, I'll bet you've experienced all three:

1. Automatic – seemingly effortless, no thinking required.
2. Semi-Automatic – requires very little mental effort.
3. Manual – effortful thinking.

An example that will lay out the differences more clearly:

Almost everything we do on a daily basis involves solving some small problem. Think about something as simple as satisfying a desire to have a sip of coffee or tea. You have your drink. It is in a paper cup with a plastic drinking lid. Without thinking about it, you are able to pick up the cup, position the drinking hole properly, take it to your lips, tip your head back, tip the cup up, and, when you feel the liquid reaching your lips, you apply the slightest suction to slurp up the hot fluids within. When enough of the liquid has entered your mouth, you tip the cup down, remove it from your lips as your head tilts down, and swallow as you place the cup back down where you found it. You did not think through any of these actions; they were automatic. You learned these steps a long time ago while drinking juice from a sippy cup. Next time you have a cup of coffee or tea think through these steps.

The above is an example of automatic problem solving, now we're going to look at a situation that requires slightly more thinking power:

Imagine you are at a soft drink dispenser. You've filled your cup and now must select the lid. There are four different sized lids to choose from, and for a moment you're not exactly sure which one to pick. It doesn't take much mental effort to select a lid and try it, but the activity does engage your active thinking slightly. You've expended very little mental effort. In fact, it is almost unnoticeable effort. This is what is called semi-automatic thought.

The third level of problem solving is effortful:

Imagine you want to come up with a machine that will automatically select the right lid, place it properly on a paper cup, and drop a straw in place with a small protective sleeve on the drinking end of the straw. Now you have to think through each activity the machine must be capable of executing: how does it detect the right cup size, how does it select which lid to use; how does it place the lid properly on the cup; how does it put the straw in, and from where do you source straws with protective sleeves on only their tops? This is effortful thinking, and you must be sufficiently motivated in order to think a problem through to its solution.

Take this problem: Together, a backboard and a basketball cost $110. The backboard costs $100 more than the basketball. How much does the basketball cost?

The funny thing about this problem is that for most people the answer $10 pops into their brain. Some people are surprised to discover that the answer is not $10. In fact, having $10 pop into your brain actually makes the problem harder to solve. It takes some mental effort to solve this very simple problem. (The correct answer is $5) This effortful 'manual' level is what Nobel Laureate Daniel Kahneman calls 'System 2'. In his model, the semi-automatic level is 'System 1'. Humans tend to favor employing System 1 to solve problems because it is efficient (low energy required) even though it is error-prone and full of biases and mis-applied heuristics (rules of thumb).

We could have used System 2 to arrive at a more accurate answer, but Kahneman repeatedly points out that the brain is a relatively "lazy" system. Why is that? The answer seems to be that as adults we are naturally wired to conserve energy.

If you think of a normal healthy young child, that mental image of a child has no sense of energy conservation. Children seem to experience a boundless supply of energy.

Physically, such children just go and go and go, until they stop and take a serious rest. They also can concentrate mental energy until it seems not to consume enough energy, and they go again physically bouncing off the walls. You don't have to tell such children to go and get some exercise. Only when they get older will they need some encouragement to move around.

For whatever reason, as we get older, we seem to conserve energy more and more jealously. For an adult over thirty years old, going out and getting some exercise takes will-power. We try to make that exercise more inviting by creating physical games, offering us increased motivation to move. Walking around a golf course is roughly equivalent to walking 4 miles, a distance recommended by health professionals for adults to walk daily. (Now you have a good reason to play a round of golf everyday, providing you walk the course.)

The third level of thinking, the manual level, is energy consuming. Reportedly, the brain consumes 20 percent of our body's energy. Some test results say that the brain uses more glucose while problem solving, but others suggest it is only a tiny amount more. Unfortunately, in looking at the research, despite using both easy and harder problems, neither type of test used in this research works the brain past the semiautomatic level of thought. For instance, there's a test called the Stroop Effect Test where the subject must identify the color of a word. In the easier version, the word 'Blue' would be colored blue, but in the harder version, the word 'Blue' will be in green or red. Since a human participant could quickly devise a strategy for dealing with this 'harder' scenario, such as only looking at the first letter of the word and checking its color, it does not represent an accurate measure of the brain activity of humans fully engaged in deep thinking.

Other examples suggest there is indeed some energy being put into effortful problem solving. Kahneman points out that one way to see this is to go walking with a colleague and ask them to multiply two numbers in their head (for instance 32 and 27). Most likely they will slow their pace or stop walking to do the math. Kahneman points out that the human brain lacks the capacity to walk and multiply such numbers simultaneously. The brain conserves energy as a reflex, and overcoming that natural response takes willpower. You can walk and solve the problem simultaneously, but you have to really want to do so.

Take this problem:

Miles Per Gallon (MPG) Problem	MPG at 75 Miles per hour	MPG at 55 Miles per hour
CAR 1	30.7	39.9
CAR 2	36.5	51.9
CAR 3	17.8	23.8
CAR 4	25.9	34.6

The drivers of the four cars in the chart above all regularly drive at 75 MPH. All four have agreed that for the next 10,000 miles on the highway they will drive at 55 MPH. Which of the four will save the most on gasoline by slowing down?

This is a marvelous problem because when I give it to groups almost everyone gives up trying to figure it out and makes an 'educated guess' usually settling in on CAR 2 because it looks like it has the biggest gap in MPG. Teams will often approach business problems with that same level of mental effort. It's not enough, and that is the problem.

65

It is the problem that must be overcome if we want our employees to be great problem solvers. They have to want to do so. They have to be motivated to think deeply. Since problems arise unpredictably, you cannot set aside an hour per week when you create some motivation and say, "Time to tackle a problem!" When a problem crops up during normal working hours, your employee must be motivated to tackle it, especially if it is a hard problem that requires a day or more of serious thought to solve.

We know from psychology and practical business experience that putting employees in that motivated position requires establishing the right working environment, with the right levels of autonomy, accountability, and motivation to foster serious problem solving. That brings us back to our sense of ownership model:

(The easiest solution to the MPG problem is to convert from Miles Per Gallon in the chart to Gallons Per 100 Miles. Then subtract one column from the other to see the difference. The larger the difference, the more is saved)

Creating Owners

W̶e know from the example organizations we discussed earlier and from the Kunkle study that creating a sense of ownership in our employees requires us first to establish their autonomy. The problem is, we don't want to give up our own control without some process to ensure that control will still exist in the company. This is the first challenge. To overcome it you are going to employ 'autonomy tools' and create an effective operating structure. This will give you both good control and effective execution. Fortunately, these tools already exist. You don't need to reinvent the wheel. Gino Wickman and others compiled a list of tried and true control tools, and we suggest that Manufacturing P.A.R. Excellence companies implement a handful of these.

You start by articulating your customer value proposition(s). When I implement the P.A.R. Excellence program with a company, I ask each member of the leadership team to write down their version of the customer value proposition(s). I've yet to have a company where everyone writes the same thing. After a bit of discussion, one team member volunteers to take all the input and write the straw-man version of the company's customer value proposition. We use it as the backboard when we want to know if something is on target. If an issue doesn't impact the customer value proposition, we'll have to be critical of why we're focused on it.

Next you establish a temporary accountability model. The way you handle accountability will change after you master the problem solving and process disciplines. To get there, you start with traditional peer-to-peer accountability in the leadership team. This accountability model requires members of the team to report to one another, rather than (or in addition to) their manager. Later, that accountability requires each individual to answer to the populations upstream and downstream of their work. This was a key insight that Morning Star Tomato Company learned and has since passed on to others.

Pat Lencioni points out that a peer-to-peer accountability model is much stronger than the one you find in the manager-subordinate relationship. To create a platform for peer-to-peer accountability, we utilize weekly tactical and quarterly strategic meetings, which I will describe shortly. In these meetings, every member commits to behaviors oriented around specific activities or aimed at specific goals. Each team member's deliverable is always a SMART (Specific, Measurable, Actionable, Realistic, and Time-bound) goal and assigned to just one individual as the responsible party. These consist of three things:

- Routine behaviors and outcomes we track on a weekly

Scoreboard.
- Short term To-Do's that come out of our problem redress process.
- And Quarterly Goals set each quarter.

Peer-to-peer accountability is profoundly powerful, providing the peers know, respect, and trust one another. It helps a great deal if they also like each other. To help make that happen, we start each meeting with a Check-In.

Lots of people start meetings with all sorts of Check-Ins. The Check-In is designed to pull people together. Each person must speak while everyone else just listens (no texting). Since everyone must say something at the start of the meeting, the Check-In establishes that it's a meeting where everyone is expected to contribute. It also gets the shy person engaged in speaking out.

While lots of companies use different Check-In topics, in ParX we prefer to have each person share something personal and good that happened since the last meeting. It has to be genuinely personal, not something like, "I had a great game of golf on Saturday, I shot a 78!" Rather something like, "Our son has been home from college for the past six months battling depression. He's improved a lot in that time, and last week, all on his own, he went out and got a job. He makes more than his two older siblings! After lots of parental worry, my wife and I are greatly relieved, and very happy for our son." In the twenty seconds it takes to say those words, your teammates have learned a lot about you and your family situation. If you do this once a week for six weeks, the team naturally pulls together as caring adults. The Check-In is a powerful tool.

The structure of the weekly meeting is influenced by

work done by Verne Harnish and Gino Wickman and I encourage teams to use this model. It is a 90 minute meeting. After the Check-In we jump right into reporting. What the team reports on are the statuses of the individual items in the three categories of deliverables.

First is the Scoreboard. The Scoreboard consists of the key weekly on-going and routine deliverables for each team member. We use the term Scoreboard rather than Scorecard because we occasionally use golf as a metaphor for parts of Manufacturing P.A.R. Excellence. If you are a weekend golfer you certainly know other golfers who play a little fast-and-loose with what score makes it onto the scorecard for each hole. Every golfer knows that declaring a 'Mulligan' means that at least one stroke is not going to make it onto the card. Another is the 'Gimme' for a short put. It's not allowed, but people do it as a courtesy because it gets you off the green more quickly. And if you know the other rules of golf, there are numerous conditions where penalty strokes should be counted but aren't. A professional golfer has every stroke counted on their scorecard while, at the same time, the score is posted publicly on the Scoreboard. We use the term Scoreboard because the numbers are 'public' to the leadership team, and the number reflects the actual performance.

In the weekly meeting, when going down the Scoreboard list, the person responsible for the current item will say, "Met," or "Did not meet." If something is tagged as "Did not meet," it goes up on our list of weekly Concerns, Issues, Problems, Ideas, and Opportunities (CIPIO List). Since the Scoreboard is distributed to every team member before the meeting and shows history, team members can see if there's a worrisome trend. Just because it makes it to the CIPIO List does not mean we will discuss it. You'll see why in a moment.

This has to be very disciplined, particularly for manufacturers. One of the hardest things for manufacturers to do is to refrain from discussing an 'issue' when it arises. Manufacturers are amazing problem solvers. When they hear an issue, the first thing they are inclined to do is to jump in and recommend a solution. In Manufacturing P.A.R. Excellence, however, we hold our fire on discussing issues until they are all on the table and we have prioritized them.

Second is the status of the To Do's list from the prior week. To Do's are solutions to problems that can be solved or advanced toward solution quickly. Typically a To Do has a completion date set for one or two weeks out. As the team goes through the To Do's, the individual responsible for each will simply say "Done!" or "Not done but on track" or "Off track." If something is "Off track," it goes up on our list of weekly Concerns, Issues, Problems, Ideas, and Opportunities (CIPIO List).

Next is the list of Quarterly Goals. Again as we go down the list, the team member responsible for the current item says, "Done!" or "On Track" or "Off Track!" If it is 'Off Track' it goes onto the CIPIO List.

The last item in the reporting section of the weekly meeting is to capture any new CIPIO item from a customer, employee, supplier, competitor, or other source. These get added to the list without discussion.

That concludes the reporting section of the meeting and

you should be about 20 minutes into the 90 minute meeting. Most of the 20 minutes has been used to add items to the CIPIO List. That list is then prioritized. Following Gino Wickman's model, you will only prioritize the two or three most important items.

The team then puts the number one Concern, Issue, Problem, Idea, or Opportunity (CIPIO) item through the redress methodology. This is one of those times when it is initially difficult for every team to discipline themselves. They will not get it right at first. Typically the meeting leader will look at the issue, declare what the real issue is and what the solution should be and then assumes that everyone sees it the same way. Instead of asking for input, the leader asks for agreement. If the meeting leader is the CEO, people will tend to nod their heads. But even if the meeting is being led by one of the other team members, this short-stop tactic eliminates the input of shy team members.

The discipline is simple and straight-forward. With each step in the problem solving methodology, you go around the table to get a verbal input from every member of the team. Each member of the team can either add to the conversation or simply say something like "Ditto" in agreement with prior comments. The reason this discipline matters is that the best problem-solvers tend to favor listening over talking. These problem-solvers are forever gathering additional information. You have to force them out of that mode and require them to speak up, even when they want more data. Encourage participants to restrict themselves to one or two sentences.

The Manufacturing P.A.R. Excellence problem solving method involves five steps:

1. First, ask how the problem as originally stated impacts the established customer value proposition(s). This is achieved by going around the room until you reach a general consensus on how the customer value proposition is sufficiently impacted for the issue to matter. If the impact isn't significant enough, you then ask why it's an issue worth discussing at the Leadership team level. There may be a good reason, and you may continue the process or otherwise decide who should own it and hand it off to that team member. As the meeting structure cascades down through the organization, perhaps the issue will be taken up by a different team.

2. Second, you go around the table getting answers from each person to the question, "What's the real issue here?" You keep going around the table until you reach an agreement on what the real issue is and rephrase it that way.

3. Next, you ask each member in turn to identify what they suppose the root cause is.

4. When you agree on that, you go around the table seeking suggestions on how to resolve the issue and then agree on a 'best' solution.

5. In the final step, a team member takes ownership of the resolution, defines what outcome or behavior will be delivered and when. If the delivery date is within three weeks, it becomes one of their To Do's. If it is a longer delivery, it becomes a Quarterly Goal.

Teams get very good at resolving problems using this methodology. I've seen teams breeze through an issue in less than two minutes. They take the attitude that the discipline is likely to get a successful solution about 99% of the time. Occasionally they will get something wrong in the process, but they don't worry because they know they'll be putting the issue back on the table soon enough if it's not properly resolved.

This disciplined methodology is hard for manufacturing teams to adopt. They are so strongly biased to jumping to solutions. It is helpful to let someone lead the discussion other than the most senior person at the table. The job of every other team member is to police the discussion. Each team member is alert to the discussion getting off-track or out-of-step with the stages of the problem solving methodology. Their job is to speak up. For example, "Excuse me, I think we should be discussing root cause right now, not solutions." By staying on-track the team will resolve issues quickly, deliberately, and precisely but it takes practice over a few weekly meetings to get good at it.

Recently, I was working with the leadership team of a company that has done very well over the past five years. They were struggling with the problem redress methodology. I asked them to identify an issue and take it through the process. The CEO picked an issue and almost immediately they went into solution mode. I sat down and took notes. Over the next 45 minutes their discussion covered at least 11 different issues. Finally, they seemed to run out of steam and look over to me. I stood up and told they I'd captured 11 different issues and pick one from the middle of the list, "Okay, who is doing what on this issue?" Nobody responded, but a couple smiled and nodded, they knew where I was going. "How about this issue," I picked another off the list, "Who owns this issue and what is going to get done and when?" Again, silence. I picked one more issue and it was clear they got the point. They had just spent 45 valuable minutes actively discussing solutions to 11 issues and none of these issues were on a path to resolution.

If they'd spent a disciplined minute on each of the steps of the problem redress methodology, they would have resolved many, if not all of their 11 issues. Instead they'd wasted 45 minutes. They then took the time to go through three issues systematically. Yes, they frequently had to get themselves back on track. However, in about an hour, they did get through the three issues resulting in clear SMART goals.

We end every meeting with a recap of the To Do's and any new quarterly goals that came out of the problem solving section of the weekly meeting. The very last thing we do in the meeting is to rate how we did in the meeting. Whenever I am conduction an session to help a company implement tools I start the meeting by laying out the agenda, capturing expectations of each attendee, and asking them to bring their '10 game'. They will rate themselves as a team on a scale of 1 to 10 (1 being 'not good', 10 indicating a great meeting). That's why we call it a Rated 10 Meeting. If an individual rates it less than a 10 (and most do), we expect a brief explanation.

We also conduct Quarterly Strategic Meetings. In those meeting we review the bigger Quarterly Goals we set up in the prior Quarterly Strategic Meeting. We review the strategy, lay out the obstacles and opportunities that need addressing in the next quarter to be on track for the year-end goals, and set new Quarterly Goals for each individual on the team. Quarterly Goals are initiatives that are in-

75

addition-to the routine deliverables that a team member is committed to. It might be something like, 'Develop a sales strategy and tactical plan for our new product XYZ'. This would likely be assigned to the head of sales and have an end-of-quarter due date. There is anecdotal evidence that the best long-term goal is a quarterly goal. Some have suggested it relates to our agrarian roots where we had to plan by the seasons, Spring, Summer, Fall, and Winter. In fact, one of the reasons Ricardo Semler's profit sharing works so well is that they distribute profits every quarter.

Once new Quarterly Goals are established, then the one-page business strategy document is updated and made available to every employee in the company. When I implement ParX with a company, we develop this business strategy one-pager during our second implementation day. See the form at the end of this section. Also, once a year we have a two day Annual Strategy Meeting. It consists of a Quarterly Meeting baked into the development of the coming year's business strategy. Typically we do a good deal Opportunities and Obstacle work in the annual meeting as well.

The Weekly Rated 10 Meetings, the Quarterly Strategic Meetings, and the Annual Strategy Meeting provide the rhythm for the organization. These three meetings create the discipline for ensuring team member accountability.

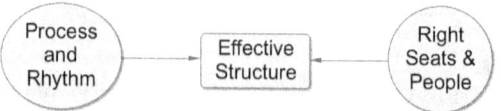

The last foundational element we put in place is the Stakeholder Chart. The method I recommend roughly follows the Accountability Chart method described in

Mike Paton and Gino Wickman's book Get A Grip starting on page 51. I won't cover that here.

A team needs to get good at the weekly meeting which means that before we add the motivation tools several weeks will pass in which the team practices the weekly meeting including getting good at the problem solving methodology.

When the team is sufficiently well practiced in the foundational tools, it is time to introduce the motivation tools. The use of peer-to-peer accountability in the weekly meeting elevates the relationship from the parent-child relationship characteristic of the manager-subordinate structure to an adult-to-adult level. This is foundational to enhancing motivation, because people do not like to be in the child role while dealing with another adult who seeks the parent role.

Annual/Quarter Goals

Goals This Year

Future date:
Revenues
Margin
Profit
Employees
Market Share

Key Deliverables for the Year

1
2
3
4
5
6
7
8

Goals This Quarter

Future date:
Revenues
Profit
Employees

Key Deliverables for the Qtr.

	What	Who
1		
2		
3		
4		
5		
6		
7		
8		
9		

Obstacles and Opportunities

1
2
3
4
5
6
7
8
9
10
11
12
13
14
15

Business Strategy

Value Proposition:

Core Purpose:

Long Term Target (e.g. 10 yrs)

Future date:
Revenues
Margin
Profit
Employees
Market Share

Medium Term Target (3 yrs)

Future date:
Revenues
Margin
Profit
Employees
Market Share

Market Niche:

Our Differentiators:

Our Guarantee:

Sales Process:

creating change

The initial structure will need some time to soak in. Typically, teams will spend four to eight weeks conducting their weekly meetings, during which time the attendees will grow together, having shared many pieces of personal good news. If a team member develops a pattern of sharing banal, non-personal news, the team will need to intervene and encourage that team member to share genuine, personal good news. The action of sharing personal good news helps to create empathy within the team, as some members of the team develop empathy faster than others and pull the rest of the team along.

During this several-week 'soak' period, team members will practice the reporting phase of the meeting. This may prove more challenging than it sounds. A recent article in the MIT Sloan Management Review reported, "*Psychologists and cognitive scientists have suggested that the brain is prone to leaping straight from a situation to a solution without pausing to define the problem clearly.*"[54] I've watched nearly every team I've worked with get sidetracked by a branch of discussion and fail to formulate a SMART resolution. The reporting section of the meeting requires the discipline of reeling in side discussions. This section of the meeting is just for reporting. The only thing anyone should be saying are things like, "Done" or "Not Done", "On Track" or "Off Track." If the issue is worth resolving, it will get prioritized in the very next section of the meeting.

The next section of the meeting often suffers from two problems:

First, team members get lazy. During the week, they begin to put aside issues in the hopes that the combined brain power of the attendees of the weekly meeting will solve those issues for them. The best team members walk into the room knowing what issue(s) they want to prioritize and have straw-man solutions in mind. It is hard to leave pride-of-authorship behind, but in problem resolution it is better to try the team's solution than to get your own way.

The second problem we raised a moment ago. We jump to solutions. The steps in problem solving need to be followed. It turns out that this is a much bigger challenge for manufacturing than practically any other industry. Manufacturers face a great many small problems each day that are solved using quick rules of thumb, or past experiences. Therefore, the problem redress discipline

54 Repenning, Nelson P., Don Kieffer, and Todd Astor. "The Most Underrated Skill in Management." MIT Sloan Management Review. March 13, 2017. Accessed Web. 23 Apr. 2017. <http://sloanreview.mit.edu/article/the-most-underrated-skill-in-management/>.

can be painful at first, especially when you go through the process and end up with the exact solution you already had in mind. In addition, the psychological phenomenon of hindsight bias can cause us to feel that the end solution was ours to begin with, especially when it is obvious in hindsight: "Of course I thought of it, it was so obvious." The team must go through the steps of disciplined problem resolution. Following the discipline is worth the investment of a comparatively small amount of time as it will periodically deliver piercing insights and perspectives that will accelerate innovation. Every team member has the job of keeping their peers on track throughout the problem redress steps.

Once the team gets good at reporting (accountability) and problem resolution, then the process of building an environment where employees will develop a sense of ownership begins. This is the stuff that mediocre managers call 'warm and fuzzy stuff' or 'touchy-feely.' This is, however, where great leaders separate themselves from mere managers. Environment building is hard work, which is why some managers denigrate it. It is much easier to order someone to do something than to put in place an environment of autonomy and a set of motivators that make the 'order' unnecessary. You won't get good problem solving from people you're ordering around. Good problem solving is a voluntary activity.

A new lieutenant arrived at the post and commanded the men to form up. "Men," he said. "I expect only one thing from you. We will get along fine provided you follow my orders to the letter." He surveyed the men. "Is that CLEAR?" "SIR, YES SIR!" replied the men. Three weeks later he approached a private.

"Private Johnson. Look at the tires on the trucks," he said. "Do they look a little low to you, private?" "Ah, yes, sir, they are indeed low, sir." "Didn't I instruct you to check the pressure in the tires every day, private?" "You did, sir. I even wrote down what the pressure was each day!" "Then pray tell me, why are the tires nearly flat?" "Well, sir," replied Johnson. "Every time I check the tires using the tire pressure gauge a little air escapes. After a while, I guess it adds up, sir."

When you tell people what to do, you're telling them not to think too hard. They know that showing some initiative will just get them into trouble eventually. So, they will try follow whatever order is given, even, "Ahead two-thirds."

Ricardo Semler pointed out that your company mission is much less important to productivity and company performance than are the individual missions of all your people. Enable their personal mission through their work, and they will be on the path to develop a sense of ownership in your company. You start that with a three-part exercise, one that enables your people to articulate their individual Personal Commercial Mission Statements. Then, you bake these into their already existing Colleague Letter of Commitments (CLoCs). See the end of this section for a shortened sample.

The Colleague Letter of Commitments is the document that ties the company's entire team together under 'contract' in line with the company value proposition(s). Here are the architecting instructions an employee would follow:

1. Start with the company's value proposition(s).

2. Establish your Personal Commercial Mission Statement.
3. Negotiate your responsibilities for behaviors and outcomes.
4. Identify one or more measurements of those key behaviors and/or outcomes.
5. Identify any developmental goals with a little help from your coworkers.
6. List your current quarter goals.
7. Ask your direct colleagues to sign your CLoC.

Initially, it is your peer group team who signs off. This team is typically defined by the hierarchy in the company and is made up of your boss and everyone who reports to your boss. Later, we will add those colleagues who are immediately upstream and downstream of your work. First, however, we need to cascade the weekly meeting structure into the rest of the organization. Later still, we'll add the Personal Commercial Identity Statements to the CLoC.

The last big initial implementation tool we introduce comes later still. Once the weekly meeting and the CLoC have been absorbed into every level of the organization, we implement the final motivational tool.

As you read through this next section, keep in mind that the underlying objective here is to help employees develop strong senses of ownership by enabling them to develop Kinship, Identity, and Meaning. Do not lose sight of this goal, as it is the primary objective. By working toward this goal, you will generate a desirable by-product, which is excellent innovation.

Colleague Letter of Commitments

Name:_____ Title_____Date:_____

Company Value Proposition(s):

Personal Commercial Identity:

Personal Commercial Mission:

My Responsibilities	CLoC Colleague	Signature
This Quarter's Goals		

My Development Plan:
Signature:_____ Date:_____

Rebel Gate

S ooner or later growth depends upon diversification. Typically diversification calls upon you to expand and change:
- what you offer;
- whom you sell to.

Both required a certain degree of innovation.[55] As a general rule, the more innovative, the better.

The thing about highly innovative companies is that most innovations come from employees. Robert Galvin and his leadership team at Motorola certainly knew this was true. And if you operate in a shop where that's not true, chances are you're not really very innovative, or highly productive, or deliver the best quality. Plus, employees who are allowed to be innovative will be far more open to ideas from outside the company than those who are frustrated in less innovative cultures.

Innovation, productivity, and quality are dependent up

55 The definition of innovation: Creating new knowledge that solves problems and provides competitive advantage.

the people who work for you. We know from many studies across many years that a worker with a deep sense of ownership is 170%-240% more productive than an unengaged worker. We also know that quality comes from caring, and it's the engaged worker who cares. And finally, innovation is a product of a engaged mind.

Creating engaged minds is clearly one opportunity worth pursuing. However, solving the sense of ownership problem only addresses half the barrier to competitive advantage. If you truly want to maximize your competeability, then addressing the more subtle and elusive other problem is critical. Whenever we do the same thing a lot, we develop mind sets.

A few years ago Dorothy Leonard-Barton published the findings from a study of innovation projects at companies including Ford and HP.[56] These firms had invested heavily in building technical competencies which ultimately defined the organization's practices and its culture. The more a change challenged the culture and those entrenched capabilities, the less able were people in the company to move forward. The dark side of core competencies is that they foster 'core rigidities'. On two important technology projects at HP, the teams had to physically and psychologically separate themselves from the rest of the company to be able to overcome these core rigidities.

Harvard Professor Donald Sull has also contributed to this research. He has shown that companies develop cognitive models, foster relationships with customers, and create

56 Leonard-Barton, Dorothy. "Core Capabilities and Core Rigidities: A Paradox in Managing New Product Development." Strat. Mgmt. J. Strategic Management Journal 13.S1 (1992): 111-25.

cultures that enable them to be successful. Unfortunately these features tend to lock the people into a specific frame of reference. The company becomes slow to respond to changes in the industry. Companies develop mind sets.

A large mobile phone manufacturer nearby employed a rigid stage-gate process. In a conversation with one of its engineers, he told me about an innovative idea a colleague of his came up with. The trouble was the idea was far enough removed from their idea (their core rigidity) of what a mobile phone should do, that they decided it did not fit. The process killed the idea in the early stage. A couple of years later someone at Apple had the same idea and it was incorporated into an iPhone.

Thus, even if you are successful with the "I think...how do we..."tool described in the next section, your decision making is still going to be influence by these well developed mental models. Like all biases, they are least evident to the people holding them. They will likely reject the change they need the most. As a CEO you face this with your people and within yourself.

Add on to this baggage that we tend to view change as risky. Risk implies a possible gain and a possible loss. People, on average, feel that to give something up they need to be paid twice as much as what they are willing to pay for it to own it.[57] As humans, we naturally overweigh risks and under value opportunity. Think of the experience you have in finding a $20 bill. You feel fortunate for a few minutes. Now think about a time when you lost a $20

---

57 Novemsky, Nathan and Daniel Kahneman (2005), "The Boundaries of Loss Aversion," Journal of Marketing Research, 42 (May 2005), 119–28.

bill. You wracked your brain trying to think where you might have put it, or where it might have fallen out of your pocket. That twenty dollars will come back and haunt you, perhaps for two or three days. Psychologically, losing a $20 bill impacts you much more than finding a $20 bill yet the financial value is the same. Humans are naturally risk averse. It's irrational but true.

Finally, to be truly innovative, you have to let your people run with the ball...a lot. The problem is this feels risky and out-of-control. Change can make us feel like we are losing control. And the more changes we have occurring, the less we feel we are in control. However, competitive advantage depends upon change.

This leaves us with four obstacles we want to overcome:
* We want to have workers who are fully engaged.
* We want a process that enables us to overcome our mental models, or at least makes our core rigidities irrelevant in making the right decision.
* We want to overcome our tendency to be risk averse, perhaps by minimizing the risk,
* Finally, we want to be in control.

A tool that specifically enables companies to overcome these issues and to become remarkably innovative is a process called Rebel Gate™. We own Rebel Gate but make it very inexpensive because unless a client company is innovative, nothing else we offer will have quite the same impact. Keep in mind that the number one objective isn't innovation, it's developing a sense of ownership.

If the only outcome Rebel Gate delivered was a deeper sense of ownership among employees, it would worth implementing. Nothing engages an employee as much as the ability to pursue an original idea. Explicit empowerment is a requirement.

At Gore "teams organize around opportunities and leaders emerge." 3M pioneered the idea of giving employees the ability to set aside time to work on special projects. Google reportedly gave its engineers 20-percent time, so that they were free to work on what they were really passionate about. Google realized that when a worker gets an idea separate from their regular jobs that worker will naturally focus 'free time' 5-10% of their time on it even if you don't sanction it. If you sanction that use of 'free-time' then you gain the most valuable thing from an employee - their engagement. Then, if the idea shows promise, other employees who've been privy to the work will join in and then it may become a real project. But even if it doesn't become a project, even if the employee has to put the idea on a shelf for a while, the engagement impact is still there. That employee will be giving the firm his or her full measure of productivity. Google's belief in empowerment can be summed up as "Give the proper tools to a group of people who like to make a difference, and they will." Google's approach is opportunity focussed. Engagement is critical to competeability.

Most company decision makers focus on the risk, not the opportunity. Where a decision-maker can form a reasonable objection, it is far less risky to say 'no' to an idea than 'yes', even when there a great reason to say 'yes'. Recently one of my partners and I attended a program on product innovation at one of the excellent universities in the Chicago area. The speaker was a professor at the university and CEO of a firm, which specializes in product development. He spent the second half of the program going through their proprietary and complex, rigid stage-gate process. My partner looked over at me and frowned. I knew exactly what he was thinking - stage-gates are focussed on risk at the expense of opportunity. Stage-gate processes are about reducing risk, but they often kill good innovation.

A key to allowing people to pursue ideas is to establish a flexible Risk-gate™ process. This processes facilitates the least expensive, but best use of resources to pass an idea through a primary risk.

One blanket way to minimize early stage risk is the "20 percent" time solution. The 20 percent time is a way to allow early stage risks to be contained to this small package of individual's time. It works well at Google because development work can be pursued by an individual or a small cooperating team. Allocating 20% time may not be practical in your company. Where your production needs eliminate the opportunity to allocate additional time to pursue such ideas Rebel Gate users will discover that employees find the time. You will not be able to stop them from spending some personal time on a project they love.

At 3M, the CEO nearly killed the idea for masking tape. Afterwards, he recognized the limitations in his own ability to recognize a good idea. He realized that an employee with a passion should be allowed to pursue an idea. This approach paid off. For example, in 1968 Spencer Silver discovered a unique, repositionable adhesive. He shopped the adhesive around within 3M without much success since the frame of reference for 3M workers was strong adhesives. Then, five years later, Art Fry, another

3M scientist, was in church singing from his hymnal and kept losing his place. He wished he had a sticky, removable bookmark that wouldn't damage the flimsy pages, and then remembered Silver's adhesive. Fry began working on the idea, and three years later, he was able to make enough of the Post-it® notes to supply 3M's corporate headquarters. The idea took hold. Three years after that, in 1980, the product launched nationally.

The key lesson here is to find ways to avoid killing ideas without breaking the bank. The mobile phone manufacturer killed an idea early, but 3M didn't.

If Art Fry had to go through a stage gate process for his hymnal bookmark the process would have required a Business Plan containing: business goals; a market analysis; financial analysis; technical evaluation; and competitive research. (These requirements are taken from the "front end" of an actual stage gate process.) You can almost hear someone kill the idea with "Look if there were any kind of market for hymnal bookmarks, someone would already be in that space. It's a non-starter."

A Rebel Gate project requires no management decision-making. An employee can establish the project. This process overcomes the company mindset issue. To provide a process for thoughtful project selection, an individual employee can only initiate 2 projects in a six month period and thus will be selective on what ideas to pursue. At this point risk is minimal since no funding is involved. But funding is often essential.

Rebel Gate establishes a flexible funding pool. It turns out that employees can be remarkably clever about finding ways to advance an idea while spending very little money. To hedge the bet on any idea, we establish a link between participation and funding.

At W. L. Gore & Associates' the approach is to allow ideas to bubble up until a team is needed to take them to the next level. As the need for additional resources increases, the team grows.

Leveraging that experience, and in the spirit of Semler's sixth principle, *Partner Promiscuously,* Rebel Gate dictates that no colleague can come to the funding pool alone; there must be at least two people. The amount they get to play with will depend on the company and the industry. For example, Two people can get up to $500. If more money is needed then a larger number of people must join the team. How you structure this depends on the funding needs in the company but it might look something like:

3 employees <= $750
4 employees <= $1,500
5 employees <= $3,000

By allowing associates to sign on to no more than two teams in a six-month period, you build in a risk control governor. Employees will want to work on teams where they believe the idea has potential. Semler's brainstorm to build a consumer version of a commercial dishwasher would likely require quite a few partners, both to move the idea itself forward, but also to fund its development. In Ricardo Semler's case no one signed on the the idea and he shelved it.

The flexible funding pool provides a very strong control. And remember, as CEO you're not paying for innovation, you're actually paying for a sense of ownership, which will return huge dividends in productivity and quality.

A flexible process enables the employees involved to establish project-specific milestones while remaining flexible about what those milestones are and who needs to be involved[58]. The employees involved identify what the next critical risk factor is, and determine what they must overcome and which approach has the smallest possible investment. Some ideas need a couple of hundred dollars to move to the next stage, but others may need thousands. The mantra for all employees is to preserve cash and look for creative ways to move an idea along without creating an unnecessary financial risk. This methodology overcomes the final obstacle, it provides very strong control.

As pointed out earlier, the biggest obstacle to innovation is mindset. By empowering any worker to take an idea forward, the mindset issue is minimized. The worker may only need to convince one other person to join in order to get funding to move to the next stage.

Inevitably an employee will come up with a great idea but is unable to get any other employee to join the project. Rebel Gate has an additional process for handling these situations which comes with the license but which I won't discuss here.

---

58 With a Rebel Gate licence you get an Excel tool that enables you to track this activity.

Behave the Change

The natural approach to making a change is to try to change your own thinking or the thinking of others and let that change drive their behavior change. Instead, behave your way to the change you want.

This kind of change isn't for most leaders. To find out how tough it is to change your own behavior try this. It's something simple with no real risk. This is a simple way to start to change the level of interaction with your workforce. It requires a simple change in your own behavior. But simple does not mean easy. This will turn out to be tougher than you might first believe. In fact, I've never known anyone who found this change easy.

As a CEO, you are the one person in the company who already knows what the CEO thinks. Many other people in the company would love to have that intelligence. Here is the problem: when you share with your subordinates what you think, they immediately stop thinking because you've done it for them. When they stop thinking, you start losing your competeability.

95

Particularly if using just one brain becomes the company's habit.

The reason you lose competitive advantage when you lose your colleagues' thinking may be obvious to you. Recall how much Ricardo Semler wanted to gloat over his employees when a competitor came out with the consumer version of a rapid dishwasher, and how sheepish he felt when that turned out to be a failure for that competitor. He realized that just being the owner of the company didn't mean that every idea he was enthusiastic about was a good one.

The behavior change is simply this: stop saying the words "I think..." (or its equivalent, "I believe...," "in my opinion...," "I suggest...") Whenever you catch yourself starting a sentence with "I think..." stop and ask a question instead. Start that question by asking, "How do we...?"

For example, instead of saying, "I think our customers expect us to package our produce in individual wrappers," say, "How do we determine how to package our product such that we will delight the customer?" By replacing "I think..." with "How do we...?", you are replacing a declarative statement with an open-ended question. You are inviting a change of behavior among your staff, and are asking for original thought, even divergent thought.

Let's assume you succeed and manage to turn a few "I think..." statements into "How do we...?" questions. Inevitably, someone will come up with an idea that's a lot different from your own. You'll be tempted to go after them, get them to change their mind. Don't. That one person is doing what you want everyone to do, to think. You're starting to get the behavior you're after. Just because this employee has an unusual idea, doesn't mean the company is impacted at all. Keep in mind that in highly innovative companies, sometimes an idea that sounds stupid at first turns out to be the best idea the company ever gets. Who would have thought there'd be a market for disposable hymnal bookmarks, much less that 50 billion of them would be sold every year.[59]

We started this monograph with the list of things that you want to be the best at in the eyes of the customer.

- Product (or service) functionality
- Packaging
- Marketing
- Pricing
- Selling
- Servicing
- Enhancing the customer's sense of identity
- Having the customer find greater meaning
- Causing the customer to like and respect your company

Let's be honest: your opinion and the opinions of your employees don't matter. It's what your customer feels that matters. With customers it's about the heart first and then the mind. Thus, when an employee has an idea you don't like, it doesn't really matter. Neither your opinion, nor your employee's opinion, matters. The question is, will the customer like it? Will it add to your competitive advantage? Will it create a blue ocean? In that circumstance, the right response is, "How can we test that idea in the least risky and least expensive way possible?" When given the

59 This, of course, is one of the most famous innovation stories—the genesis of 3M's Post-It® Notes

challenge, employees can be amazingly clever and frugal when it comes to opportunities to develop and test their own ideas[60].

---

60 One of the tools we provide in Manufacturing P.A.R. Excellence™ is a Rebel Gate™ described earlier in this monograph.

Last Word

I started this monograph supposing someone might have said, "I can run your business better than you can!" As I suggested you'd probably think, 'Hold on a second here. You don't know my business, my products, my people, my industry, my competitors, or me. How could you possibly think you could do this better than me?"

You're right, nobody can run your business better than you do, except for you.

That doesn't mean you should do it alone. Over my career I've kept track of things that work and things that did not work well when it comes to leading people, and getting the best ideas from them. I have also studied this with passion and have been diligent in uncovering why things work. If you don't know why something works it's hard to manage it. That has lead to many tens of thousands of pages of study in business, psychology and behavioral economics.

As a result, I know why some tools recommended in books like Traction actually don't drive performance the way the authors think they do. Some very common tools actual work against you and I've jettisoned those.

Manufacturing P.A.R. Excellence salvages the best tools from these methodologies and adds other tried-and-true tools to accurately target the outcomes we all seek. What that means is while you know your business very well, and the ParX tool kit puts process around the change you want, together you'll crush it.

In this monograph I've given you just a sketch of the tools in Manufacturing P.A.R. Excellence. That was intentional. I do not want you to try to self-implement the ParX operating methodology. As self-serving as that might sound, there is actually a good motive behind that position. The leaders who have done the best job of making their companies great have sought outside advice. As Ralph Stayer put it, *"The day-to-day pressures of running the business continually distracted me from what I wanted to create. I needed someone whose specific job was to help me focus on learning my new leadership role."*[61]

The truth is, a change like this makes it tough for the CEO to walk the talk. Under the pressures of the day-to-day management, CEOs easily fall back into old habits. To the team that looks like someone who can't walk the talk. It undermines the effort. A more successful strategy is to bring in the person who does the talking. Then everyone on the leadership team struggles together to get the walking right, including the CEO.

Over the last few years, my partner and I have helped companies implement the Entrepreneurial Operating System. And in the last couple of years I have had the

---

61 Belasco, James A., and Ralph C. Stayer. Flight of the Buffalo: Soaring to Excellence, Learning to Let Employees Lead. New York: Warner, 1993. P.27

opportunity to spend time with a few manufacturers who self-implemented the system. They all think they did a good job putting the system in place and every one of them is wrong. Because CEOs don't have the time to get the depth of understanding and training that an professional implementer does, they will naturally miss some of the important nuances. They customize the system for their own use and in the process lose something critically important. One CEO changed the issue resolution process which did not allow the person in the know to raise a different point of view. One consequence was that the business suffered a tough 2016, which could have been avoided.

When it comes to self-implementing Manufacturing P.A.R. Excellence there is even a bigger reason not to do so. Among the significant changes that have to take hold are changes to the habits of the CEO. Having an implementer in the room enables the leadership team to police the team's activities including the CEO's own activities. If the CEO is driving the implementation personally, then that key aspect will not be there since, without a referee, subordinate executives will be very cautious in challenging the CEO. The worst case is where the CEO does not think this is true for his or her team.

Best advice is: just use an implementer! Implementers are all highly experienced executives trained in the nuances of P.A.R. Excellence.